HORRIBLE SCIENCE

EVOLVE OR DIE

PHIL GATES

illustrated by
TONY DE SAULLES

■SCHOLASTIC

Visit Tony De Saulles at
www.tonydesaulles.co.uk

Scholastic Children's Books,
Euston House, 24 Eversholt Street,
London, NW1 1DB, UK

A division of Scholastic Ltd
London ~ New York ~ Toronto ~ Sydney ~ Auckland
Mexico City ~ New Delhi ~ Hong Kong

First published in the UK by Scholastic Ltd, 1999
This edition published 2008

ISBN 978 1407 10535 2

Printed and bound by CPI Group (UK) Ltd, Croydon, CR0 4YY

19 20

CONTENTS

Phil Gates is an extraordinary man. Not only is he a successful writer and respected scientist, he has won several awards for his sculptures made from wet tissues. His hobbies include standing in rock pools in the freezing cold and playing snooker. He hopes to win a game before his next birthday.

Other books written by Phil include *Interview with a Dinosaur, Molluscs! Are they really boring?* and *A Mosquito called Fred.*

Tony De Saulles picked up his crayons when he was still in nappies and has been doodling ever since. He takes Horrible Science very seriously and even agreed to sketch *Megachasma pelagious* – the sixth largest shark in the world. Fortunately, he has made a full recovery.

When he's not out with his sketchpad, Tony likes to write poetry and play squash, though he hasn't written any poetry about squash yet.

INTRODUCTION

Biology lessons can be totally mind-boggling. So many amazing creatures to consider. So many tongue-twisting names to remember. It's utterly unfair of teachers to expect us to learn all the jaw-breaking scientific jargon that they insist on using to describe the simplest things.

But there's a much better way to learn about biology, if teachers would only use it. All they need to do is to stop ranting about so many sickening scientific facts, and turn it all into a story. So instead of beginning a lesson by saying "Today we're going to learn about the chemical reactions in chloroplasts" – which sends any self-respecting class into a deep sleep almost instantly – they ought to start with the words, "Once upon a time…" That would work wonders for turning their pupils into better biologists. Everyone likes a good story, so the whole class would hang on to their every word.

The thing that biology teachers need to remember is that life is a story. Life had an incredible beginning when the first creatures crept around on the ocean floor, 3,500 million years ago. Since then it's been through some terrible times. Sometimes it's been almost wiped out completely by awesome accidents. Sometimes it's tried out unbelievable experiments, producing crazy creatures like Hallucigenia (see page 98).

There's a name for the story of life on Earth. It's called evolution. It's a story that's been going on now for 3,500 million years, and no one has any idea when it will end.

Evolution is an epic adventure, on a scale that even Hollywood film directors could never contemplate. It's got disasters, surprises, villains, heroes, horror – and even sometimes a happy ending or two along the way.

Evolution is simply amazing. It's incredible. So here's the full story. Read it, and biology lessons will never be quite the same again.

A HIGH-SPEED HISTORY OF LIFE ON EARTH

Earth can be a horribly hostile habitat sometimes. Since life first appeared here, our planet's weather has often been appalling. It's been sizzling hot and dry as dust, teeth-chatteringly cold and covered in ice, or dismally wet and waterlogged – sometimes for millions of years at a time. And at one time or another our planet has been surrounded by poisonous gases, bombarded by asteroids from outer space and showered with invisible (but deadly) ultraviolet rays.

But somehow life has struggled through. It's done it by evolving – by constantly changing, a little bit at a time. Lucky life forms, that just happened to be born with the best body bits for living in horribly hostile environments, thrived, bred and produced descendants that are well adapted for survival too. The unluckier life forms, that weren't so well equipped, died out.

This is what scientists call evolution. It's a bit like fashion. You've got to move with the times, or – as scientists say – you've got to evolve.

But fashion changes every few months. Evolution is horribly slow. It can take millions of years for something interesting – like an extra set of legs, or a pair of wings – to evolve.

Evolutionary time is even longer than an average school lesson, so let's speed it up a bit. Here's a lightning-fast history of life on Earth. Hold tight – over the next few pages we'll be whizzing along at over 150 million years per second.

Millions of years ago

4,500
Earth formed from the remains of exploding star. Everything horribly hot. Volcanoes everywhere. No water. No air. No life.

4,000
Planet cooling down. Water forms. It rains. That makes a change!

3,500
Atmosphere smells like a gigantic fart – it's full of sulphurous gases. An evil-smelling chemical cocktail in the oceans reacts to build an amazing molecule called deoxyribonucleic acid (dee-oxy-ry-bow-nuk-lay-ik acid) – but you can call it DNA.[1]

1 Molecules, by the way, are made when simple chemicals combine to make more complicated ones. The DNA molecule is inside all living things and can make copies of itself (see page 52).

3,000

Conditions on the planet keep changing, so DNA molecules must keep evolving to survive  in hostile habitats. Some devious DNA slips into a tough survival suit and becomes the first nasty bacterium. These bugs breed until they cover every surface in a layer of slime. They feed on sulphur, so the atmosphere soon smells like the inside of a pair of your old trainers on a hot day.

DNA MOLECULE

2,000

All this activity needs energy. Some bacteria turn green, because they're crammed full of a chemical called chlorophyll, which can trap energy from the sun. Instead of developing a suntan, these bacteria use the sun's rays to turn water and carbon dioxide into sugars for their food. This means that they give off oxygen, which poisons most of the other sulphur-feeding bacteria. They retreat into deep oceans and down into stinking muds, where they still survive today.

1,000

At last! After 3,500 million years of evolution, something that looks like an animal. Primitive worms crawl around under water.

570

Suddenly evolution goes mad. Hordes of weird wildlife evolve. Then some of it dies out again. That's evolution for you: two steps forward, one step back. Luckily some life survives, so evolution doesn't have to start again from the very beginning.

500

 Make way for the terrible trilobites, which look like underwater woodlice but grow up to 50 times larger.

440

Plants invade the land, which slowly goes green. Seas full of savage, three-metre-long sea scorpions called Eurypterids (you-rip-ter-rids). The first fish with jaws evolve (until now, all they could do was give you a nasty suck). Some fish evolve legs and begin to crawl on to land.

410

The sea is seething with an amazing variety of fish species – an angler's paradise. Life on land gets noisy, because croaking amphibians (distant relatives of frogs and newts) are everywhere. Not a good time to go collecting tadpoles, though – some of the amphibians are as big as crocodiles. Life takes off when the first flying insects evolve.

10

365

Atmosphere like a steamy bathroom. Plants just love this warmth and wetness. Swampy forests of giant ferns, hiding demon dragonflies (as big as birds), monstrous millipedes and the first reptiles.

290

Phew, wot a scorcher! It's getting hotter and drier now. Revolting reptiles begin to take over from artful amphibians. After 210 million years of trundling around on the seabed, the trilobites' luck runs out – it's extinction for them, because sea levels drop and the edges of their ocean habitat dry out.

230

Those cute little reptiles that first put in an appearance 135 million years ago are bigger and fiercer now. Yes, that's right – they've evolved into dinosaurs. Evolution invents dinosaurs for every purpose. Giant herbivores like Brachiosaurus, that could eat a whole tree for breakfast; vicious Velociraptors that hunted in packs; terrible Tyrannosaurus Rex, the largest predator of them all. Rapacious reptiles also ruled most in the air and sea. Pterosaurs soared overhead, while Ichthyosaurs and giant turtles cruised the oceans. No, this wasn't a good time to be small and edible.

210

Flowers flourish. All sorts of insects evolve, in horrible hordes. Small furry animals called mammals appear. They're smart and  nimble. They need to be, or they'll be trampled by dinosaurs.

140

Birds evolve from small running dinosaurs. Oceans full of awesome ammonites, which look like octopuses wrapped up in a flat curly shell.

65

Whoops! Dinosaurs become extinct. Once the dinosaurs have gone, the smarter furry mammals turn nasty – now they're Planet Earth's most deadly predators.

2

Horrible humans evolve. Regular Ice Ages make their teeth chatter. Mammoths become very hairy to keep warm, but they still die out. Did human hunters turn them all into fur coats and mammoth burgers?

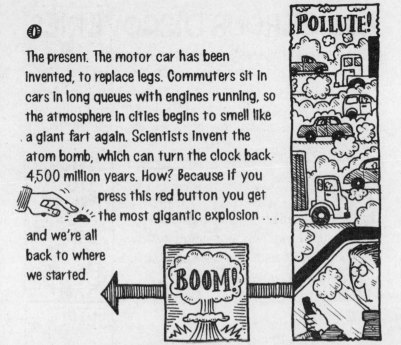

The present. The motor car has been invented, to replace legs. Commuters sit in cars in long queues with engines running, so the atmosphere in cities begins to smell like a giant fart again. Scientists invent the atom bomb, which can turn the clock back 4,500 million years. How? Because if you press this red button you get the most gigantic explosion ... and we're all back to where we started.

POLLUTE!

BOOM!

Still with me? Good. Keep up.

So here we are today. Human beings: masters of Planet Earth.

How did we get here?

Where did we come from?

What happened over the last 4,500 million years to turn a lifeless, fiery planet into a green and watery home for millions of animal and plant species?

Big questions.

Scientists can answer some of them, but it takes quite a while. So stock up on some crisps, sweets and fizzy drinks to give yourself stamina, make yourself comfortable and get ready for the answers to some horribly hard scientific questions.

DANGEROUS DISCOVERIES

Back in the early 1800s most people expected religious leaders to provide answers to really big questions. So if you'd asked an Archbishop or a Cardinal how life began, they'd have told you to read the Bible. Different religions had different explanations, but they were mostly based on the same idea:

In the Christian religion, which most British people followed at the time, God created Heaven and Earth, then filled Earth with all the living things. It's all there in the Bible, in Genesis Chapter One.

You should read it – it's a horribly good story. If you do, you'll see that people were a bit of an afterthought, made on the sixth and last day of Creation.

That must have been a busy week. One clergyman even went to the trouble of working out exactly when it happened...

Bet you never knew!

In 1620, Archbishop Ussher worked out when the world began. He did it by carefully reading through the Bible and adding up the ages of all the characters in its pages. Right back to the first humans – Adam and Eve – in Genesis Chapter One. He calculated that God created Adam and Eve at 9 am on Sunday 23 October 4004 BC.

Today, modern scientific tests prove that our planet was created after the explosion of a star, about 4,500 million years ago. The Earth is nearly a million times older than Bishop Ussher's estimate. And a lot can happen in 4,500 million years!

NEW IDEAS COME FLOODING IN...

Bishops found that geologists – scientists who study rocks – were terrible troublemakers. They'd been digging up fossils of ancient animals, buried in rock. Some were hideously different from any creature that anyone had ever seen before.

And funnily enough, amongst the fossils of these ugly beasts there wasn't a sign of a human skeleton to be found. Not even the half-chewed bits of an unfortunate human that the beasts had eaten for breakfast. It began to look as though humans were newcomers on Earth, arriving after almost everything else was already here.

Even before Darwin (see page 19) thought of the idea, there were a few scientists who had already begun to suspect that everything alive had evolved from extinct ancestors. But most were far too scared to say so. A few brave scientists did speak out, but people were usually shocked by what they had to say. And clergymen still had some explanations up their sleeve.

Fossils are the remains of ancient animals that became extinct. New ones must have evolved to replace them.

Nonsense. Fossils are the remains of all the animals that didn't get on board Noah's Ark quickly enough, and were drowned in The Flood. GLUG! GASP! They prove that the story of Noah is true.

16

Then how come, when you dig down through layers of rock, you find dozens of layers of dead animals? They all became extinct at different times. Does that mean there were lots of floods and lots of Noah's Arks?

Ha-ha, no! It's God's little joke. He put them there to confuse you.

It looks like evolution to me. Newer rocks at the surface have different fossils than the older rocks lower down. Animals that were fossilized recently must have evolved from older ones.

Prove it!

If living things really did evolve, scientists would have to come up with a convincing theory to explain how they did it. Across the English Channel, one flamboyant Frenchman thought he had the answer…

Hall of fame: Jean Baptiste Pierre Antoine de Monet, Chevalier de Lamarck (1744–1829)

Nationality: French

Lamarck – as he used to call himself, in case he fell asleep before he got to the end of his name – was a distinguished soldier who decided to put down his sword, pick up a dissecting knife and become a zoologist. After exploring the innards of all sorts of animals Lamarck came up with a shocking theory of evolution, that went something like this...

If an animal has to do the same task over and over again, its body gradually changes to make the task easier. So if a deer reaches higher and higher into trees for food, day after day, its neck will gradually stretch as it gets older.

If a deer's neck grows longer during its lifetime, all its babies will be born with long necks too. In this way, long-necked giraffes could have eventually evolved from short-necked deer that had to stretch to reach food.

When you think about it, this is a daft idea. It would mean that all Olympic athletes who trained hard and ended up with strong, muscular bodies would have children that could be Olympic athletes without bothering to practise as much.

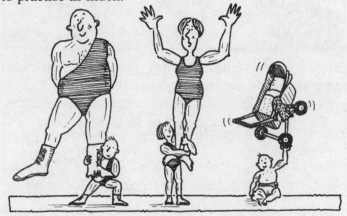

Most scientists didn't think much of Lamarck's ideas either. They laughed at him. But at least he had a theory that tried to explain the way that living things evolved, even if it was wrong. By doing that, he encouraged another great scientist to search for the right one. Enter...

Hall of fame: Charles Darwin (1809–1882)
Nationality: British

Charles Darwin was one of the greatest scientists who ever lived. He was the grandson of Josiah Wedgwood – a world-famous pottery manufacturer – and married his cousin, Emma Wedgwood.

So pottery ran in the family, and some say that Charles was a bit of a crackpot himself. His curiosity made him do strange things...

He played musical instruments to worms to see if they could hear different sounds.

He fed roast meat to insect-eating plants called sundews, to find out how they digested their food.

But above all else, Darwin is remembered today for discovering how evolution really works.

TEST YOUR TEACHER ON THESE DARWINIAN DETAILS

Ask them to guess which of these are true or false.

1 Which of these books did Darwin write?
a) *The Origin of Species*
b) *The Lost World*
c) *Evolve or Die*

2 Darwin's favourite plant was…
a) the meat-eating Venus's fly-trap
b) squirting cucumbers
c) cauliflower

3 Darwin was the world's leading expert on…
a) barnacles

b) fleas

c) monkeys

4 One day, when he was out collecting beetles, he saw one that he wanted, but he already had one in each hand. Did he...

a) put them under his hat and grab it?

b) put one of the beetles in his mouth, leaving one hand free to grab it?

c) stomp on it with his welly?

5 Which of the following is named after Darwin:

a) A city in Australia?

b) A frog that keeps its babies in its mouth?

c) A sweet-scented plant that's used to make perfume?

Answers: 1 a) is true, **b)** and **c)** are false. He also wrote loads of other books, on coral reefs, climbing plants, orchids, earthworms and chickens, pigeons and other domestic animals. **2 a)** is true, **b)** and **c)** are false. He called Venus's fly-trap "the most wonderful plant in the world", because its leaves are like jaws that snap shut and catch flies that land on them. **3 a)** is true, **b)** and **c)** are false. If you needed to know anything about barnacles, Darwin was the bloke to ask. Until he took a detailed look at barnacles, people believed that they were close relatives of snails. He proved that their closest relatives were really crabs. **4 b)** is true, **a)** and **c)** are false. The beetle that he put in his mouth was a bombardier beetle, that squirted a hot liquid out of its bum and burnt his tongue, so he had to spit it out. **5** They're all named after Darwin. Baby Darwin frogs jump into their mum's mouth when there's danger about.

21

Charles wasn't much good at passing exams at college. He preferred to spend his time studying beetles and other creepy-crawlies. When he left university he signed up as a ship's naturalist on a five-year voyage around the world, where his knowledge of natural history might be useful.

DARWIN'S DANGEROUS IDEA

Darwin was just 22 years old when he set off on his voyage around the world to study wildlife. He wasn't much of a sailor, and spent quite a bit of time being seasick.

On their way down to South America they made plenty of stops along the way. The captain was busy making maps of the coast, which left Darwin with spare time to go ashore and add to his creepy-crawly collection.

They sailed around the treacherous Cape Horn, at the tip of South America, and through some of the worst weather that ships ever come across.

The ship, HMS *Beagle*, was only 30 metres long, but no fewer than 74 crew members lived on her for five years.

It's hard to imagine what life on the *Beagle* was like, but it might have been something like this…

The year is 1835, and HMS Beagle is pitching and rolling in the waves as it crosses the southern Pacific Ocean. Seated in the cabin are two men. One is a naval officer, resplendent in gold braid. The other, an amiable looking bloke with bushy whiskers and a balding head.

Charles Darwin belched contentedly and leaned back in his chair. He picked at a morsel of tortoise flesh that had stuck between his teeth.

"That made a tasty meal, Captain Fitzroy," he said. "But I wish we could have taken the giant tortoises home alive."

Fitzroy sighed the deep sigh of a man whose patience was running out. For four and a half years now he'd shared his cramped cabin with Darwin. Sometimes he wished he'd never let this eccentric naturalist aboard his ship. Everywhere Fitzroy looked there were dead, goggle-eyed animals peering at him from pickling jars. Bunches of parrot skins swung from a hook over his head and frequently knocked his hat askew. Piles of pressed plants slid off tables every time the ship rolled in the heavy swell. Whenever he tried to pace the deck he stubbed his toe on fossil bones of giant extinct animals that Darwin had collected.

"I'm sorry, Darwin, but there's just no room for any more live animals. Look around you. Where could we put six giant tortoises?"

Darwin eyed Fitzroy's hammock, but said nothing. His gaze shifted idly to the pile of empty tortoiseshells. Each one came from a different island in the group of Galapagos Islands that they had just left behind. Suddenly Darwin noticed something that he hadn't spotted before. Each shell had a slightly different pattern. *Why?* he wondered.

He pondered the question for some time before a thunderous thought hit him. His jaw dropped. His eyes glazed over. The jars of preserved specimens swam before his eyes.

The penny finally dropped. It was the Galapagos tortoises that set Darwin's mind racing. Could it be that a single type of tortoise had originally landed on one island, swimming across from the coast of South America? And could it be that its descendants changed a bit, every time they'd colonized a new island? Each island was a bit different, with different kinds of plants growing on it, so maybe the tortoises that lived on each island needed to be a little bit different too.

Suddenly, it all seemed to make sense. He thought back to the birds that he'd seen on the islands. There were little brown finches on every island, and each island had its own special versions of these birds. They were all basically the same, but each species on each island had a slightly different beak shape. Perhaps they'd all evolved from the same species which had arrived on one island then evolved a bit when it spread to the others.

GALAPAGOS GUIDE BOOK

The Spanish discovered these islands in 1535. They found giant tortoises there, so they called them the Galapagos Islands after *galapago*, the Spanish word for tortoise.

The islands were created by undersea volcanic eruptions, 960 km west of the coast of Ecuador in South America. Volcanoes still erupt there quite often.

The islands were once a favourite holiday destination for pirates and buccaneers, who came for a bit of rest and relaxation after raiding South American cities. The peckish pirates were particularly partial to a giant tortoise barbecue on the beach.

Evolve or die fact file

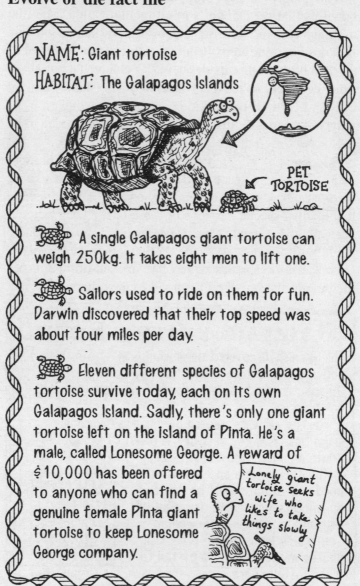

NAME: Giant tortoise

HABITAT: The Galapagos Islands

PET TORTOISE

A single Galapagos giant tortoise can weigh 250kg. It takes eight men to lift one.

Sailors used to ride on them for fun. Darwin discovered that their top speed was about four miles per day.

Eleven different species of Galapagos tortoise survive today, each on its own Galapagos Island. Sadly, there's only one giant tortoise left on the island of Pinta. He's a male, called Lonesome George. A reward of $10,000 has been offered to anyone who can find a genuine female Pinta giant tortoise to keep Lonesome George company.

Lonely giant tortoise seeks wife who likes to take things slowly

As they sailed home Darwin became certain that you could tell which island a tortoise came from by the pattern on its shell. They probably had other tell-tale features too, but unfortunately it was too late to find out. They'd loaded some live giant tortoises on board HMS *Beagle*, and he and Fitzroy had eaten them.

Still, it looked suspiciously like all the different types of tortoise had evolved from a single ancestor. Darwin began to wonder whether all kinds of living things had evolved in the same sort of way.

The differences between the tortoises were quite small, but later he began to wonder whether evolution could explain bigger differences between species too? Could fish have wriggled out of the sea, grown legs and evolved into amphibians like newts and frogs?

And what if men had evolved from the same ancestors as monkeys?

Now that *was* a dangerous theory. Darwin knew that the Church wouldn't like the idea that men and apes might be close cousins.

AN AWESOME IDEA

When Darwin returned to England he settled down to write about his trip. As he wrote, he remembered all the strange plants and animals that he'd seen. He was sure that modern life forms must have evolved from ancient ancestors.

That meant that you could trace the ancestors of all living things on Earth today back to those slimy life forms that slithered in the primaeval soup of Earth's ancient seas!

And humans and chimpanzees must have evolved from the same distant, extinct ancestor.

Men and monkeys share the same ancestors, but they've evolved different skills.

Darwin could only come to one conclusion. Living things weren't all created at once by God in 4004 BC. Today's plants and animals evolved very slowly from ancient ancestors.

It was a horribly big idea. And he knew it would get him into big trouble. So Darwin decided to wait a while before he told anyone what he thought.

He waited a week.

He waited a month.

He waited a year.

In the end it took him *twenty* years to pluck up enough courage to write his famous book on evolution. It was called *The Origin of Species*[1] and became an instant bestseller. People had heard rumours that it contained some scandalous ideas, so they rushed to the book shops to buy a copy. Every single copy was sold on the day that it appeared in 1859.

There was a reason why Darwin finally decided to publish his ideas in 1859. Someone else was about to beat him to it. Alfred Russell Wallace (1823–1913), a naturalist who made a living collecting animal specimens on Pacific Islands and selling them to museums, had also realized that living things must have evolved from one another. And he wrote to Darwin to tell him about his bright idea. Darwin wasn't too pleased – he'd thought of it first, and no scientist ever became famous by being the second person to make a discovery. So Darwin sat down and wrote his book as fast as he could.

1 Actually, it's not. Its full title is – take a deep breath – *The Origin of Species by means of Natural Selection or The Preservation of Favoured Races in the Struggle for Life. The Origin of Species* is just easier to say.

To be fair, Darwin and Wallace's ideas were announced at a gathering of some of the world's eminent scientists at the same time, but few people remember poor old Wallace. Darwin got all the glory. Science can be horribly tough.

THE GLOVES COME OFF...

Darwin's book made him famous, but he had to put up with a torrent of criticism from people who hated his ideas. His followers were called Evolutionists. His opponents became known as Creationists, because they believed every word of the story of Creation in the Bible.

They had some ding-dong rows. Darwin couldn't stand public arguments. He stayed at home most of the time and left it to his Evolutionist friends to flatten the opposition.

Their most famous fight took place at the meeting of the British Association for the Advancement of Science in the University Museum at Oxford on 30 June 1860.

Sir, you say that we are all descended from apes. So tell me, was your grandmother or your grandfather a monkey?

Sir, I would prefer to have a miserable ape for a grandfather than a man like you, who uses his influential position to mock scientific discussion

The war of words between the Creationists and Evolutionists didn't always end happily. One famous supporter of Bishop "Soapy Sam" Wilberforce came to a tragic end.

He was Captain Fitzroy, who had commanded HMS *Beagle* during Darwin's voyage around the world and shared a cabin with the naturalist. Like many Victorians, he believed every word of the Creation story in the Bible. He was horrified that he'd accidentally helped Darwin to collect evidence for his vile evolutionary theory and helped to cast doubt on people's religious beliefs.

One Sunday morning on 30 April 1865 he locked himself in his study and killed himself, by cutting his own throat. You might think that's a bit much, but it just goes to show how much people hated the idea of having monkeys in the family.

Poor old Fitzroy wasn't the only one who wouldn't believe Darwin's theory. Scores of sceptical scientists pointed out that creatures had to have some way of passing on their best body bits to their babies. It was no good being brilliantly equipped for life on Earth if they couldn't pass on their finest features to their descendants before they died.

...TO MY DAUGHTER I LEAVE MY EXCELLENT EYESIGHT AND STRONG TEETH

Otherwise the features that made them so successful would die out with them. Nothing would ever change: evolution wouldn't happen.

Darwin didn't come up with a convincing answer to this question.

After all, even Charles Darwin didn't have all the answers. But other scientists were able to pick up his ideas and test them out for themselves, by studying fossils (see pages 72–90) and some of the animals and insects that are still around today. Cute, cuddly animals like rabbits. Or small, vicious insects like mosquitoes. Slowly, but surely, a picture began to emerge. It wasn't always a pretty picture but, finally, scientists could see how the theory of evolution actually worked. So cover up, slap on some insect repellent and prepare yourself for an encounter with some ... murderous mosquitoes!

MURDEROUS MOSQUITOES

Evolution was a big, new idea. Scientists needed to come up with some pretty impressive evidence if they wanted to convince everyone that they were right.

Luckily, scientists can prove that evolution really does happen, because they can see species change before their eyes. Big changes in evolution take millions of years, but small changes can be amazingly quick.

Evolve or die fact file

NAME: Malarial mosquito

HOME: Anywhere that's horribly hot and wet.

MOST FRIGHTENING FEATURE: Spreads a dreadful disease called malaria. The mosquitoes suck your blood, then squirt squirming parasites into your veins. These give you a fever with horribly high temperatures, and they can even attack your brain.

Scientists have invented all kinds of drugs to kill the malarial parasites that mosquitoes carry. At first they're usually successful, but a few parasites always survive. This is because there are small differences between individual parasites. There are always a lucky few that are naturally protected from the chemical poisons.

These vile variations survive in someone's body and are passed around when another mosquito sucks their blood and then moves on to a new victim.

So then it's back to the drawing board for the scientists, in search of another drug that will wipe out this new version of their old enemy.

If it wasn't for the fact that malarial parasites are constantly changing, we might have got rid of this disgusting disease long ago. The trouble is, the parasites keep evolving and stay one step ahead of scientists.

Bet you never knew!
- *When characteristics of individual living things change slightly, they're called mutants. The changes are called mutations.*
- *Most of the time mutations aren't much use to their owners. A cauliflower is just a mutant cabbage, with a horrible-looking head of white flower buds that never open properly. Cauliflowers only survive because people who like to eat vegetables that look like brains deliberately grow them. From a cauliflower's point of view, flowers that never open are a dead loss, so cauliflowers can't survive without human help.*
- *Sometimes mutations are useful. When animals change – when people start attacking them with chemical sprays, or when the climate gets hotter or colder, or when finding food gets tougher – then the right kind of mutation can be very useful indeed. Then a mutant with better body bits might survive. And if it survives, it'll breed – leaving lots of copies of itself – just like the mutant malaria parasites. So then a new, slightly different version of the species has evolved.*

This is exactly what happened to polar bears, when they first arrived in the Arctic. Originally the bears had brown fur, but over time some of them evolved into bears with white fur. But not all. Those bears that still had brown fur found that it was more difficult for them to sneak up on seals in the snow, so they were less able to feed themselves … and slowly died out.

RABBITS' RECIPE FOR SUCCESS
Rabbits breed like, well, like rabbits, really. *Very* fast. Each one can produce around 50 baby bunnies each year.

The population of animals in a species tends to increase as long as there's plenty of food, water and somewhere to live. When these start to run out, life gets tough. Animals have to compete against other members of their own species in order to survive.

Suppose you were a rabbit. OK, so it's not that simple, but give it a try. Which would you rather be? A brown rabbit, a black rabbit or a white rabbit?

Choose your colour now, then see long you'd survive: Imagine…

a) You're foraging for nice juicy vegetables in a ploughed field.

b) You're out at night – are you protected from danger?

c) Humans are hunting for rabbit fur. Are you safe?

d) There's thick snow on the ground, and the stoats are sniffing around for a tasty snack.

Survival scores:
a) Two years if you are a brown rabbit – you'll blend in easily against the field. One year if you're black – you don't stand out too much. Almost no time at all if you're white – you'll stick out like a sore thumb and make easy prey for passing stoats.
b) Two years if you're brown or black. You won't be easily snapped up by passing owls. It's bad news if you're white, though. They'll see you easily, so you won't have long to live.
c) Two years if you're brown. Your fur is too dull for a fashionable fur coat. Almost no time at all for black or white rabbits, though. Your handsome fur is far too attractive.
d) Two years if you're white. You blend perfectly with the snow. But brown or black rabbits won't survive long – the stoats are on their tails in no time.

So now, if you add up your total survival scores, you can work out how long you'd live.
For a brown rabbit, it comes to a total of six years. And remember, you can produce 50 babies each year, so this is long enough to leave behind at least 300 bunnies that look exactly like you, and are just as successful.

For a black rabbit, it comes to just two years … only long enough to leave behind 100 baby bunnies, if you're lucky, but their survival chances aren't as good as their brown cousins.

And as for white rabbits … well, if they're lucky they can expect to live for two years too, so they'll leave behind 100 white rabbits that will be hoping that it snows more often!

So it's easy to see why black or white rabbits are rare. If you chose to be a boring old brown rabbit, you'll have survived these conditions best of all. But what if the climate changed? Suppose it got colder and snow was on the ground all year round. It'd be a different story then, your white cousin would become fittest and survive more successfully.

In any rabbit population, most animals will share similar characteristics, but there will always be a few rabbits with mutations that might come in handy. They can vary in all sorts of ways – they might have longer guts, for example, so they can digest food more easily – always useful if you spend all day chewing grass.

TEST YOUR TEACHER

Most scientific words sound horribly difficult, but actually the language scientists use is supposed to make complicated things easier to understand. Ask your teacher what coprophagous (cop-roff-a-gus) means. Is it:

1 TO EAT DUNG?　**2** TO EAT POLICEMEN?　**3** THE COFFIN THAT EGYPTIAN PHARAOHS ARE BURIED IN?

Answer: 1 Rabbits are coprophagous, because their guts aren't long enough to digest their food on its first trip through their bodies. So they send it around again by eating their own dung.

Scientists love making up weird words like coprophagous. It's the easiest way to describe this particular rabbit habit. But most people don't understand them, so they just call it "dung-eating" – but that doesn't sound half as impressive, does it?

Mutants that are slightly better at getting the things they need survive and thrive and breed. Gradually they start to take over. Evolution has happened and the species has changed a bit.

Scientists sometimes call this natural selection because in wild plants and animals the individuals that succeed are the ones that are lucky enough to inherit a winning set of characteristics from their parents.

Conditions on Earth are always changing slightly, so animals and plants with new, useful mutations do better as time passes. If mutations never happened, then plants and animals couldn't evolve to suit the changing conditions, and they would eventually become extinct. So if you want to survive, it's evolve – or die!

"AAAAAH - HE'S GOT HIS MOTHER'S NOSE"

All living things have small differences – mutations – that are passed on from their parents. You've probably noticed how certain features tend to run in families. Don't you just hate it when this happens…?

YOU'RE THE SPITTING IMAGE OF YOUR GREAT-UNCLE ALBERT

ER YEAH, THANKS AUNTY

Sadly, all kids have to put up with these kinds of comparisons. Aunts, uncles and grannies just can't stop themselves. People have always marvelled at the way characteristics are passed down through families. And they have always wondered why it happens. One of the first people to come up with an answer was…

Hall of fame: Hippocrates (460–??? BC. No one is quite sure when he died.) Nationality: Greek
Hippocrates is famous for all sorts of things. He's sometimes called "the father of medicine" because he invented ways of finding out what was wrong with sick people, and tried to find cures. Even today doctors swear a Hippocratic Oath, which is a promise that they'll do their best for their patients and won't do anything to harm them.

Hippocrates came up with a half-baked hypothesis to explain how parents pass on their characteristics to their children…

Hippocrates got it horribly wrong. After all, when you mix the colours of a paint box together you always get the same muddy colour when you've finished. All the individual colours disappear into the mixture. So if characteristics from both parents were just mixed together in their children, everyone in the family would soon look more or less the same.

If a tall father and a short mother had children, they would all be medium height, and then all *their* children would be medium height, and all *their* children would be medium height. Borr-ring!

Darwin knew there was something slightly dodgy with this idea. His theory of evolution depended on individuals passing on their different features to their children. If they didn't, mutants couldn't pass on their useful body bits to their children. Evolution wouldn't happen.

Hippocrates' explanation lasted for 2,300 years. It was time for a new one, and the person who produced it was…

Hall of fame: Gregor Mendel (1822–1884)
Nationality: Austrian, (but born in the country that's now called the Czech Republic)

Mendel came from a peasant family, so getting him a decent education was pretty tough on them. His parents knew their son was a clever lad, though, and managed to get enough money together to send him to school and then on to university. Eventually Mendel became a monk. But there was something very different about him. Mendel was a monk with a passion for plants. Peas in particular. He spent most of his time in the garden.

Just like Darwin, he set out on a voyage of discovery – but Gregor only got as far as the vegetable plot at the bottom of the garden. Every year between 1856 and 1863 he filled his garden with peas: 30,000 plants altogether. Tall ones, short ones, yellow ones, green ones, wrinkled ones, smooth ones. Then he cross pollinated the flowers with a paintbrush, collected the seeds that they produced and sowed them again.

Dare you discover ... how flowers work?
You will need:
A small paintbrush
Some flower seeds – nasturtiums are ideal for this experiment
A flower pot
Some seed compost to sow the seeds in

What you do:

Sow the seeds, water them and wait for them to grow and flower. When the flowers open, use the paintbrush to collect some pollen grains. As you may know, these are the bits that bees collect and carry from flower to flower. Use the paintbrush to put the pollen on the flower's stigmas, where it will fertilize and make the seeds form. Then all you need to do is plant the seeds to make them germinate and grow.

Here's a picture to remind you what's what and where's where in a flower:

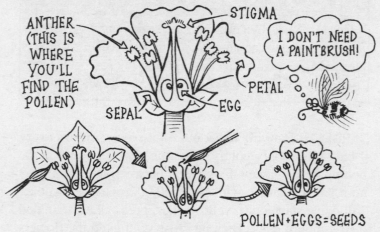

ANTHER (THIS IS WHERE YOU'LL FIND THE POLLEN)

STIGMA

I DON'T NEED A PAINTBRUSH!

PETAL

SEPAL

EGG

POLLEN + EGGS = SEEDS

Mendel took over the bees' job and carried the pollen from flower to flower, so he'd know exactly which plants were paired together.

Once the flowers turned to seeds Mendel spent all his spare time sorting them out into different types and counting them. Then he sowed the seeds again and counted all the different kinds of plants that grew from them – wrinkled seeds, smooth seeds, tall plants and short plants. Then he got out his paintbrush and cross-pollinated these plants all over again. Mendel was a monk with a mission. He'd find out how living things passed on their characteristics, no matter how long it took.

One day, after years and years of tedious work, Mendel was struck by a thunderous thought (at long last!).

He worked out that each characteristic must be passed on in a tiny particle according to an amazing mathematical law that never changed. And if he wanted to know what the next generation would look like, all he had to do was to look at each parent's features and remember some simple rules.

MENDEL'S GOLDEN RULES

1 Characteristics such as the colour of a flower in plants, and nose size or knobbly knees in humans, are passed on from parents to their children through invisible particles inside their cells.

2 A different particle carries the instructions for each characteristic.

3 The particles work in pairs, and one of each pair comes from each parent.

4 Particles exist in two different forms. Particles can be dominant, which means that their effects always show up. Or they can be recessive, which means that the effects of a recessive particle can be hidden behind the effects of a dominant one. But if two recessive particles pair up, then their effects always show up in the plant or animal that carries them.

It works like this…

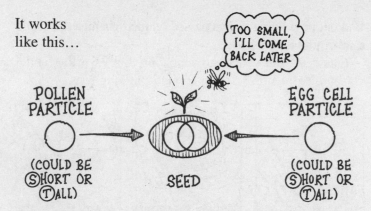

POLLEN PARTICLE

(COULD BE ⓢHORT OR ⓉALL)

SEED

EGG CELL PARTICLE

(COULD BE ⓢHORT OR ⓉALL)

TOO SMALL, I'LL COME BACK LATER

In this example, remember these rules: tall particles are dominant, short particles are recessive.

So…

A tall particle paired with a tall particle produces a tall plant.

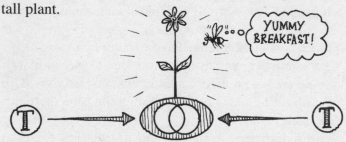

YUMMY BREAKFAST!

A tall particle paired with a short particle produces a tall plant (the short particle is recessive, so its effects are hidden behind the tall one).

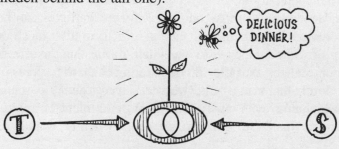

DELICIOUS DINNER!

A short particle paired with a short particle produces a short plant.

FANTASTIC FACTS

- Today we call Mendel's particles genes. All the characteristics of all living things are controlled by genes, which are passed on from parents to children. They're like a set of instructions carried inside the cells of your body.
- Even a tiny, simple organism like a bacterium is controlled by over 10,000 genes. It takes around 25,000 genes to form the complete set of instructions for making something as complicated as a human.
- Mutations happen when genes change. Mutant genes are nature's way of changing the instructions slightly and inventing new body bits.

Mendel's discovery started a whole new science, called genetics. And a whole new bunch of scientists, called geneticists.

But geneticists couldn't really study genes properly until they knew where they were. By the beginning of the twentieth century, geneticists were tearing their hair out trying to find these pesky particles. To their surprise, they soon realized that they'd been staring at them for years.

Well, that's not quite true. You can't actually see a single gene, even with a really powerful microscope. It's far too small. But you can see genes when thousands of them are collected together in one place. And the place to look is inside a cell.

CYTOPLASM = SNOT-LIKE SLIME

NUCLEUS =
THE INFORMATION
CENTRE, WHERE
THE GENES
ARE, SENDING OUT
A STREAM OF
INSTRUCTIONS
TO THE CELL

COME ON, CELL, GET A MOVE ON!

MITOCHONDRIA = POWER STATIONS THAT BREAK DOWN FOOD AND TURN IT INTO ENERGY

SEVEN SENSATIONAL FACTS ABOUT CELLS

1 Insects, plants, animals, bacteria … from ants to elephants, all living things are made up of cells.

2 Cells are usually tiny. If you lined up 40 average-sized plant cells they would only just stretch across the head of a pin.

3 If humans had the same cells as plants, we'd be green! Plant cells each have special green, shiny chloroplasts to turn sunlight, water and carbon dioxide into food.

4 Did you have a nice fried egg for breakfast this morning? Actually, you ate a fried giant cell! Birds' eggs are special, they are made up of a single cell covered in a hard shell that helps them survive outside their owner's body.

CAN I HAVE BEANS WITH MY GIANT BIRD'S CELL PLEASE, MUM?

5 Ostrich eggs weigh about one and a half kilogrammes, so they hold the record for the largest cells in the world.
6 If you took your clothes off and stood in front of a mirror, everything you'd see would be dead. All the cells on the outside of your skin have died and are falling off. But you'll be relieved to know that the cells under your skin are dividing all the time to make brand new cells. You get a nice new layer of skin about every six weeks!

NOT TONIGHT, JOE – I'M WAITING FOR MY NEW SKIN TO COME THROUGH

7 The dandruff on your teacher's collar is made up of dead cells. When the cells were alive the genes inside them contained all the information to create an exact copy of your teacher.

INCREDIBLE CHROMOSOMES

Even way back in Mendel's day, scientists had some pretty powerful microscopes. They were strong enough to reveal the nucleus of the cell. And sometimes in place of the nucleus they identified long worm-shaped things. They called the wormy bits chromosomes. *Chroma* means coloured and *soma* means body – they are slightly coloured compared with cells, which you can see through.

Chromosomes are pretty incredible:

1 Chromosomes carry all your genes, like a long string of sausages.

2 They spend most of their time hanging around in pairs. Different animals and plants have different numbers of chromosomes.

You have got 46 (23 pairs).

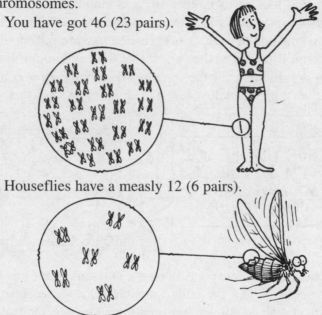

Houseflies have a measly 12 (6 pairs).

But the adder's tongue fern holds the record with an incredible 1,260 (630 pairs). No one knows why it needs so many!

3 When your skin grows, and its cells divide, weird things happen to the chromosomes inside them. The chromosomes divide too, so that each new cell carries a full set of instructions that tells it everything it needs to know about being part of you.

4 A human female egg cell and a male sperm cell carry only 23 chromosomes each. When they join together to make a baby, the two sets of chromosomes make up a full set of 46 chromosomes, but half the chromosomes come from the mother and half from the father.

5 So your genes come half from your mum and half from your dad. The sets of genes or chromosomes in egg or sperm cells are all slightly different, and no one can ever know which egg and sperm cells will join together to make a new person. So, unless you have an identical twin, there's nobody anywhere in the world who is *exactly* like you.

A POTTED HISTORY OF GENETICS

These days scientists know a lot more about genes than Mendel did. They even know what they're made of, thanks to…

Hall of fame: James Dewey Watson (1928–)
Nationality: American

Watson grew up in Chicago, USA. Even as a young lad he showed amazing brain power and entered the University of Chicago at the tender age of 15!

He was an amazing 25 years old (most scientists are really ancient) when he and his pal Francis discovered DNA.

Francis Crick (1916–2004) Nationality: British

When he was a kid, Crick's parents bought him a children's encyclopedia and reading it made him decide he wanted to be a scientist. But he was worried that by the time he grew up, everything would already have been discovered. Little did he know, that along with Watson, he would make one of the greatest discoveries ever – how DNA was structured.

Watson and Crick worked together at Cambridge University. Later James Watson spent most of his time helping to make a map of all the genes that produce the instructions for making a human. Francis Crick moved on to finding out how brains work, but they're both most famous for discovering the struture of DNA, the magic molecule of life, that first turned up in those pongy primaeval oceans, 3,500 million years ago. They won a Nobel Prize for it.

A HORRIBLE THOUGHT...

The DNA that existed inside the first bacteria 3,500 million years ago still survives inside us, in a mutated form. It's been inside slimy worms and giant sea scorpions, pterodactyls and eventually people. All the time it's been mutating, building different body bits around itself to carry it safely into the next generation. All the different animals that have lived on Earth have been built by DNA molecules. And we're just the latest creatures that have evolved to carry that ancient DNA.

That means that we're really just slaves that carry this amazing molecule. Life evolved just to make sure that genes made of DNA molecules survived.

A British scientist, Professor Richard Dawkins (1941-) had an idea about the DNA molecule. He called his idea the Selfish Gene theory.

SO LONG AS DNA IS PASSED ON IT DOES NOT MATTER WHO OR WHAT GETS HURT IN THE PROCESS. GENES DON'T CARE ABOUT SUFFERING, BECAUSE THEY DON'T CARE ABOUT ANYTHING.

He suggests that all plants and animals are really just slaves to this amazing molecule. We only exist to make sure genes made of DNA molecules survive. Other scientists disagree – of course!

AHA! I SEE YOU HAVE A NEW BATCH OF DNA MOLECULES IN PRODUCTION!

ER, WELL THAT'S ONE WAY OF PUTTING IT!

Darwin's evolutionary theory really took off once scientists discovered that evolution happens because genes change, so that better body bits can be passed on from generation to generation. But it didn't come up with all the answers. If one species could evolve into a new one, that meant that scientists urgently needed to answer a new and horribly difficult question.

Where did one species finish, and a new one begin?

SPECIES SPOTTING

Darwin's theory of evolution is all about the ways in which old species change into new ones. So what – exactly – is a species? You might be sorry you asked that question.

It's a well-known fact that if you ask two scientists the same question you'll get at least three different answers. If you're lucky.

IS CHOCOLATE GOOD FOR YOU?

CERTAINLY – FULL OF ENERGY – JUST WHAT AN ACTIVE YOUNGSTER LIKE YOU NEEDS

CERTAINLY NOT! IT ROTS YOUR TEETH.

If you are unlucky they'll answer your question with another question.

WHAT'S THE BIGGEST MAMMAL?

IN THE SEA OR ON THE LAND? IN THE SEA IT'S THE BLUE WHALE, ON LAND IT'S THE AFRICAN ELEPHANT

It's also a well-known fact that if you ask the same scientist the same question twice, you'll probably get two different answers.

Scientists are like that. Can't make up their minds. Always looking for that final piece of evidence that will provide conclusive proof. Always changing their minds. You've got to expect this really, because they are always discovering new things.

Why do you need to know what a species is? Because the next bit of this story is horribly tricky.

The trouble is that – even today – scientists can't agree on exactly how to describe a species. This is a bit of a disadvantage if you are trying to explain how species evolve.

Confused? So are they. It's a horrible mess, but they're doing their best to sort it out.

CAN YOU SPOT A SPECIES?

Easy-peasy?

You must be joking!

You might think that you can identify most species just by looking at them closely. After all, you can tell most wild flowers apart by the shape of their leaves and the colour of their flowers.

And you can tell different snakes apart by the patterns on their bodies.

And you can identify most fish by their shapes, sizes and colours – and even by the way they behave:

This is all very convenient. The world would be a dangerous place for people who couldn't tell domestic cats from cougars, just by looking at them. If you can't, just be very careful next time you stroke a cat.

But (and you'll have guessed by now that "but" is one of scientists' favourite words) the only reliable way to be sure that two species are different is if you can be certain that they can't breed with one another. And the trouble is that a surprising number of species that look different enough to be different species can actually interbreed..

Take domestic cats and fierce Scottish wildcats, for example. They can breed with one another and their kittens have characteristics of both species – they'll bite your fingers off, then purr with pleasure.

Animals that interbreed like this are a real problem for scientists who study evolution, because you can't be sure where one species finishes and another begins. Take, for example, the ridiculous situation with the ruddy duck and its Spanish relative, the white-headed duck…

RUDDY DUCKS ON RAMPAGE

White-headed ducks hadn't seen their ruddy relatives for tens of thousands of years, so it was a happy day when Sir Peter Scott brought them back together again.

Sir Peter brought ruddy ducks from America and released them in a British bird reserve.

BREEDING BRILLIANT
The ruddy ducks settled down really quickly, and soon the pitter-patter of tiny ruddy feet

meant that they were here to stay. Some even fancied seeing the sights of Europe, and flew over to Spain, where their relatives - the white-headed ducks - live.

RED FACED
But then things started to go horribly wrong. If Sir Peter Scott were alive today, he'd

certainly be red in the face when he realized the chaos his ruddy ducks have caused. Unfortunately, the ruddy duck seems to think that it belongs to the white-headed duck family. The families look quite different, but when white-headed ducks and ruddy ducks get together, they only produce ruddy babies. There's not a white head to be seen. So it may not be long before the last white-headed duck kicks the bucket!

ROTTEN LUCK FOR RUDDY DUCKS
The white-headed duck was already rare, so now bird experts are raring to get at the ruddy duck - and they've got their rifles ready. So must we bid the ruddy ducks bye bye, or will they see the hunters coming - and duck?

The ruddy duck and white-headed duck aren't really separate species, even though they look different. They're one species that's on the way to splitting into two separate species, but hasn't quite got there yet. Which just goes to prove that old Darwin was dead right – species weren't all created at once and they haven't stayed the same since the beginning of time. They're always changing, a little bit at a time. Ruddy ducks and white-headed ducks breed together to produce ducklings that grow up looking like ruddy ducks and can breed with both bewildered parents. Biologists call them hybrids.

So there you have it. You asked: "What's a species?" As any decent scientist would say, a species is either:

a) a group of creatures that look similar.

b) a group of creatures that can't interbreed with any other groups of creatures.

Two answers. What did you expect? This is science! Scientific ideas evolve too, just like life.

TEST YOUR TEACHER

See if your teacher can spot a true species by asking them which of these horrible hybrids is too ridiculous to be real?

a) Tigons have a lionness for a mother and a tiger for a father.

b) When a zebra mates with a donkey, you get a zonkey.

c) The barking pussyfish is a hybrid between a catfish and a dogfish.

Answers: a) true b) true c) ridiculous

Hybrids create horrible problems for scientists who are trying to explain how evolution works. Species are formed when one species evolves into another, new one – but how can the new species become different if it keeps interbreeding with the old one? Somehow the old species and the new species have got to become completely separate. It's a mind-boggling problem – a problem, in fact, that has boggled many minds since Darwin's day.

Luckily, scientists have come up with an explanation for the way that one species separates into two. It's a bit like the way that English and American people have come to speak different versions of the same language.

Four hundred years ago, when the first boatload of English people sailed to America, they all spoke the same kind of English.

But since then, Americans and English people have evolved separate words for the same things.

Of course, English and American people haven't split into separate species. But imagine what it must be like for animals that have been separated for millions of years, then meet up again. They can't understand each other's squeaks, squawks and roars, so they just ignore each other and behave like separate species.

In nature, all sorts of barriers can break up a species into small groups of creatures that begin to evolve separately. They can be separated by:

● rivers, earthquakes or volcanic eruptions;

● mountain ranges;
● sinking land, which leaves animals stranded on islands above the waves;

● breaking bridges. Snowy Siberia (in Asia) was once joined to Arctic Alaska (in America) by a bridge of land that sunk beneath the sea. Once a single species of bear could stroll between the continents. Now two types of bear have evolved – grizzly bears in North America, black bears in Asia – separated by the sea;

- rising land, which leaves marine animals separated.

Sometimes animals can become castaways. They can get carried out to sea and end up stranded on islands. Remember those Galapagos giant tortoises, and Darwin's finches that he found on the Galapagos Islands?

TEST YOUR TEACHER

See if your teacher can work out the answer to this primaeval problem.

Mesosaurs were reptiles that spent their time swimming and sunbathing in fresh water lagoons about 300 million years ago.

These days they're extinct, so you only find their fossils, deep down in coalmines in Africa and South America.

So how come you find identical mesosaur fossils on two different continents, separated by thousands of miles of salty sea?

1 They swam backwards and forwards across the Atlantic Ocean, so the same species lived on both sides.

2 They floated across on logs.

3 They walked across on a land bridge that's disappeared below the waves.

4 It's just a coincidence. Identical mesosaurs evolved separately, at the same time, in each continent.

5 South America and Africa were joined together 300 million years ago when mesosaurs lived. Much later, they split in two and drifted apart, carrying away some of the fossilized remains of mesosaurs on each continent.

Hall of fame: Alfred Lothar Wegener (1880–1930) Nationality: German

Alfred Wegener led a colourful life. When he finished his studies at Heidelberg University, starry-eyed Alfred became an astronomer. Then he became a balloonist and made a record-breaking 52-hour balloon flight to test scientific instruments. Still looking for adventure, he became a polar explorer and trekked off into the frozen wastes of Greenland, once nearly coming to grief when the ice broke up under his expedition's feet. Alfred saw plenty of weather, one way and another – during his balloon flights, and drifting around on icebergs – so he eventually settled down to become a professor of meteorology – the posh name for the scientific study of weather.

That was when he had a brainwave. Earth's continents, he decided, were moving under our feet. Not very fast, but they were definitely moving. It was obvious, really.

When Wegener looked at the atlas, he could see that South America and Africa had once been joined together.

YOU NEED ONLY LOOK AT THE MAPS OF THE TWO CONTINENTS TO SEE THAT I'M RIGHT. THE EAST COAST OF SOUTH AMERICA FITS QUITE SNUGLY INTO THE WEST COAST OF AFRICA. THEY'VE SPLIT AND DRIFTED APART

Wegener called his theory "continental drift".

THE CENTRE OF THE EARTH IS SO HOT THAT ALL THE ROCKS HAVE MELTED INTO A WHITE-HOT LIQUID. SOMETIMES THIS MOLTEN MASS BREAKS THROUGH THE SOLID CRUST ON THE OUTSIDE – AS A VOLCANO

ALL THE CONTINENTS FLOAT ON A MOLTEN CORE AND DRIFT AROUND. SOMETIMES THEY SPLIT APART TO MAKE SEPARATE CONTINENTS. SOMETIMES THEY JOIN TOGETHER TO FORM A NEW ONE

CLAPTRAP! RUBBISH! TWADDLE! TOSH!

In 1930 Wegener set off on another expedition, to Greenland. Sadly, he never came back and didn't live to see the day his theory was proved right. Modern-day geologists have proved beyond doubt that Earth's continents really have been slowly moving for millions of years.

Dare you discover ... how continents are like custard?

Continental drift is hard to imagine because it's so slow. Even slower than evolution. But here's an experiment to show how it works without having to wait several years for the result.

You will need:
a large bowl of warm, runny custard
two pieces of cling film
three flavours of potato crisps (cheese and onion, salt and vinegar and prawn cocktail)
a small heavy object – like a key

What you do:
1 Lay the two pieces of cling film on the custard. Then place the crisps on the cling film as shown:

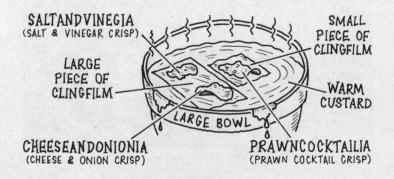

SALTANDVINEGIA
(SALT & VINEGAR CRISP)

SMALL PIECE OF CLINGFILM

LARGE PIECE OF CLINGFILM

WARM CUSTARD

LARGE BOWL

CHEESEANDONIONIA
(CHEESE & ONION CRISP)

PRAWNCOCKTAILIA
(PRAWN COCKTAIL CRISP)

2 You have now created the weird planet of "Custard World". Here, three continents float on a sea of custard, supported by drifting plates of cling film.

3 Now choose a spot in between Saltandvinegia and Cheeseandonionia and put the key on the cling film, so that it begins to sink into the molten core of the custard.

And now:
* *Marvel!* at the way Saltandvinegia and Cheeseandonionia move closer together and their crispy surfaces collide as they're drawn together by the sinking cling film!
* *Gasp!* in amazement as you watch Cheeseandonionia and Prawncocktailia drift apart!
* *Tremble!* with excitement as you watch the lake of molten custard between Cheeseandonionia and Prawncocktailia solidify in the cold air, adding new solid skin to the edge of the cling film continent!

CONTINENTAL DRIFT

Continental drift works in similar ways on Planet Earth and on Custard World. Continents like Africa, South America and Australia are plates of rock that float on the molten core of the Earth.

MOLTEN CORE

PLATE

NOW

EARTH'S CRUST RISING

FINE! OCEAN

GAP BETWEEN CONTINENTS WIDENS

NOW

EARTH'S CRUST SINKING

YIKES!

GAP BETWEEN CONTINENTS IS REDUCING

Mountain ranges are the result of colliding continents. The land has nowhere to go but up as the plates of rock push against each other.

MILLIONS OF YEARS AGO INDIA COLLIDED WITH ASIA

HIMALAYAS

INDIA

TEST YOUR TEACHER

Africa and South America are still drifting apart. How fast are they moving?

a) 2 miles per year
b) 20 miles per year
c) 3 metres per year
d) about 5 cm per year

So what's all this got to do with the way that species are formed? Well, when continents split apart, separate groups of animals in a species find themselves marooned on different continents, and each group begins to evolve a bit differently. And this explains why...

- There are elephants, giraffes and lions in Africa, but you won't find any of them in South America. And you won't find South American llamas and jaguars in Africa either. These animals evolved in the places they live today *after* the continents had drifted apart and became separated by the South Atlantic.

200 MILLION YEARS AGO

TODAY

IT'S LIKE A JIGSAW

- There are fossils of the *same* plants and animals in ancient rocks in South America, Australia and Antarctica. These three continents were once all joined together. Now they've split apart and are separated by sea.

- Early explorers found fossils of sea creatures on mountain tops. The rock that the mountains are made from formed beneath the sea. Sea creatures turned into fossils in the slimy ooze on the sea floor. Then continents collided, forcing the Earth's crust to buckle like a wrinkled rug, and the sea floor was pushed up in the air, to form mountains.

- Some of the fossils you find in Britain are the remains of animals like corals, that lived in warm, tropical seas. That's because millions of years ago Britain started out south of the equator, and had been slowly drifting northwards – towards the North Pole – ever since. There are no living corals like this around our coasts today – the water is far too cold – but the fossils are a reminder of the tropical seas that once surrounded our islands.

So that's how new species are formed. Groups of animals get separated, and they evolve into a new species.

But when new species form, the old ones often die out. And we wouldn't know that they'd ever existed, if it wasn't for the fact that some of them have turned to stone…

FASCINATING FOSSILS

Rows about evolution rage on to this day. Like all scientific ideas, Darwin's theory of evolution convinced a lot of people, but for a time that was all it was – a brilliant theory. Just like the theory of continental drift it needed more proof! And ever since Darwin died, scientists all over the world have been tracking down clues to the horrible history of life on Earth.

Scientists know all about dinosaurs and other extinct animals because their remains are buried in the earth, preserved as fossils. You've certainly heard of dinosaurs, you've probably read quite a bit about them, but did you know that all sorts of other eerie creatures crawled over our planet millions of years ago? Scientists find fossils to piece the facts together.

FANTASTIC FOSSIL FACTS

1 When ancient animals died they were often covered by layers of mud, especially if they lived in water. Their soft bits usually rotted away quickly, but their hard teeth, claws and bones often turned to stone after they were buried. They became fossils.

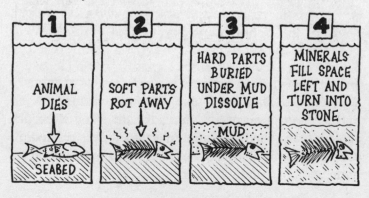

2 The word fossil has evolved from a Latin word – fossilis – which means "dug up".

3 When people first discovered fossils they weren't sure what they'd found. One theory was that these strange creatures that looked like nothing on Earth could only have come from one place – Hell! They firmly believed that fossils were bits of devils and dragons. Since then, science has shown that these bits of mythical beasts are really fossilized parts of animals that had once roamed the Earth.

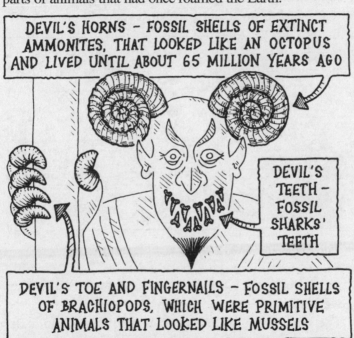

DEVIL'S HORNS – FOSSIL SHELLS OF EXTINCT AMMONITES, THAT LOOKED LIKE AN OCTOPUS AND LIVED UNTIL ABOUT 65 MILLION YEARS AGO

DEVIL'S TEETH – FOSSIL SHARKS' TEETH

DEVIL'S TOE AND FINGERNAILS – FOSSIL SHELLS OF BRACHIOPODS, WHICH WERE PRIMITIVE ANIMALS THAT LOOKED LIKE MUSSELS

4 Belemnites (bell-em-nights) are bullet-shaped fossils that we now know were once the hard parts of extinct animals that looked like squid. When they were first found, people thought that they were made by thunderbolts hurled at the earth by the gods.

5 People who study fossils are called palaeontologists (pally-on-tol-o-gists). They try to rebuild the skeletons of ancient animals from the fossil bones that they excavate. Sometimes they're lucky and find a complete skeleton, but often they only find a few scattered bones. Reconstructing a fossil skeleton is a bit like doing a giant jigsaw puzzle, and it can be horribly confusing if pieces of the puzzle are just a bag of bones. It took several attempts to put *Tyrannosaurus rex* together, and some palaeontologists still argue about whether they've got it right.

They certainly make mistakes sometimes:

- Bits of fossil trees have been given different scientific names because palaeontologists didn't realize they were all part of the same plant.
- The same mix-ups have happened with fossil animals. At first, when scientists found three kinds of weird, 500-million-year-old fossils they thought they were different species, and gave them each a name. Finally they realized that they all fitted together, to make *Anomalocaris* – a strange undersea predator that lived on the sea floor about 500 million years ago.

REVOLTING RECONSTRUCTIONS

With a bit of practice palaeontologists can become really skilled at rebuilding fossil animals, and some of these long-lost creatures have turned out to be spine-chilling predators...

Name: EURYPTERUS (you-rip-ter-us), the giant water scorpion.

Size: About as long as an alligator.

Lived: 435 million years ago.

Most frightening features: Ferocious. So paddling at the seaside when *Eurypterus* was around would have been horribly hazardous.

Name: DIATRYMA (dy-er-try-mer), the devil bird.

Size: A flightless bird, over two metres tall, that strutted around the grassy plains of Europe and North America.

Lived: 40 million years ago.

Most frightening features: Probably ate horses. It had a sharp-edged beak like a giant can-opener that could have sliced you in half!

75

Name: SMILODON (smile-o-don),
the sabre-toothed tiger.

Size: A bit bigger than today's tigers.

Lived: 16,000 years ago

Most frightening features: Lurked in bushes
and ambushed anything that came too close.
Meeting smilodon was nothing to smile about.
Its name means
"knife tooth" and its
horrible grin would
reveal two giant teeth
that were as long as
swords, and every bit
as dangerous.

PETRIFIED POO

To a scientist who studies evolution, there's nothing so
fascinating as a lump of fossil faeces (fee-sees). Faeces,
by the way, is a posh scientific name for a pile of poo.

Fortunately, not many animals manage to digest all the
food that they eat. Some interesting food fragments are
often left in the dollops of dung that they leave behind. If this
foul faeces finds itself in the right conditions – like a bog
where there's no oxygen for bacteria that would normally
eat it – then the poo gets preserved. It becomes a fossil.

Many a pile of steaming dinosaur poo has turned into
solid rock, full of interesting plant fragments. Millions of
years after an ancient animal's last meal, scientists can
explore its petrified poo and find out who or what it ate.

Scientists called these lumps of fossil faeces

"coprolites". And some coprolites are unbelievably ancient. One discovery dates from the Silurian period, over 400 million years ago. It is about the size of a mouse dropping and it probably belonged to an animal like a large millipede, which was one of the first animals to crawl from the sea and live on land.

HOW SCIENTISTS DEAL WITH DINOSAUR DUNG
(in four very careful steps)

1 First, they find a coprolite. They need a beady pair of eyes for spotting millipede poo – it's a specialist job – but giant lumps of dinosaur doings are hard to miss. They sometimes turn up alongside piles of fossil dinosaur bones.

2 Now they stew the poo in hydrofluoric acid – very nasty stuff. Hydrofluoric acid eats through just about anything – stone, metal, even school dinners – everything, in fact, except the tough outer covering of plants, called cutin.

3 Then they sort through the sludge of plant bits that's left behind.

4 Finally, they peer at them down a microscope, taking a close look at the left-overs from the dinosaur's last meal. When scientists did this with 400-million-year-old millipede poo they discovered that:

- prehistoric plants were completely different from modern ones, because the fragments of their leaves didn't match anything you find today!
- these ancient plants grew from minute, dust-like spores instead of large seeds.

Bet you never knew!

During his round-the-world trip Charles Darwin collected loads of plant and animal fossils. His most spectacular discoveries were the fossil skeletons of a giant South American ground sloth called Megatherium. *It looked a bit like an overgrown bear. If* Megatherium *hadn't become extinct it would have been able to peer through the first-floor bedroom windows of today's houses, just by rearing up on its hind legs. Nothing to worry about, though – it only ate leaves.*

Darwin was sure that today's sloths, which are only about the size of a ten-year-old child and live in the South American jungles, were related to these extinct monsters from the past.

FANTASTIC FREE-RANGE DINO EGGS

When palaeontologists find a really good fossil they sometimes take it along to a local hospital, and borrow a CAT scanner to see what's inside. CAT stands for computerized axial tomography, and a CAT scanner is machine that lets doctors see what's going on inside their patients. It also lets palaeontologists see inside lumps of rock that may contain an important fossil.

Palaeontologists are always digging up amazing fossils. Dinosaur eggs are quite common in some parts of the world. Put them in a CAT scanner and you can sometimes even see baby dinosaur bones inside.

Recently a fossil *Oviraptor* dinosaur was actually found sitting on its nest. It turned up in 1995, in the Gobi Desert in Mongolia. People used to think that *Oviraptor* was a thief, stealing and eating eggs of other dinosaurs, because it was often found around dinosaur nest sites. Then they discovered this unlucky specimen, which must have been sitting on its own nest, protecting its eggs – just like today's ostriches do – when it was buried in a sand-storm.

Dinosaurs have a reputation for being horribly fierce but it looks like this *Oviraptor* was a bit of a heroine, buried alive while she tried to save her babies.

COULD YOU BE A PALAEONTOLOGIST?

You need...
A hammer
Goggles
Tons of patience!

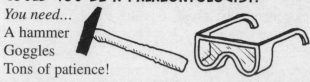

ANY LUCK?

NOT YET, BUT I'VE FOUND A CAVE

Where to look...
If you're going to be a palaeontologist you'd better learn to recognize rocks that contain fossils. Here's how:

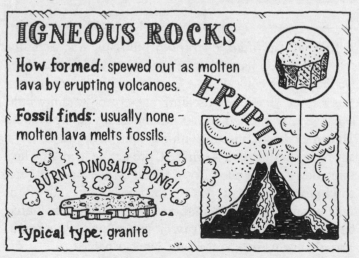

IGNEOUS ROCKS

How formed: spewed out as molten lava by erupting volcanoes.

Fossil finds: usually none – molten lava melts fossils.

ERUPT!

BURNT DINOSAUR PONG!

Typical type: granite

80

SEDIMENTARY ROCKS

How formed: produced when particles of sand, mud or skeletons of tiny sea creatures cover dead plants and animals, then slowly turn everything to rock.

Fossil finds: full of fossils

Typical types: sandstone, limestone and chalk

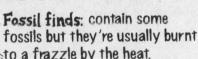

METAMORPHIC ROCKS

How formed: from sedimentary or igneous rocks that have been cooked at horribly high temperatures by volcanic activity and turned into different kinds of rock.

Fossil finds: contain some fossils but they're usually burnt to a frazzle by the heat.

Typical types: marble, made when limestone is heated under great pressure.

So your best bet is to search in sedimentary rocks. As you chip down through layers that took millions of years to form, you should find trapped plants and animals from the past. It's a bit like taking a trip back through time, and it can be terribly tedious. It might take hours, days, months or even years to find anything interesting. But if you're really, really lucky, you might just come across a fossil bed...

Fossil beds were formed when dead animals and plants were washed into piles by currents in ancient rivers or seas. They're heaps of fossils all bundled together in a huge lump of rock. So you *could* find hundreds of fossils, all at once.

What to do:
If you *do* find a fossil, you'll need to chip away really carefully with your hammer around the edges.

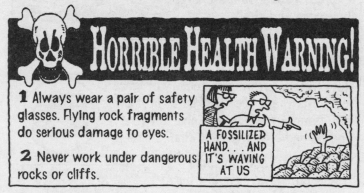

HORRIBLE HEALTH WARNING!

1 Always wear a pair of safety glasses. Flying rock fragments do serious damage to eyes.

2 Never work under dangerous rocks or cliffs.

A FOSSILIZED HAND. . . AND IT'S WAVING AT US

If all this chipping gets too boring you could fake some fossils instead.

FOSSIL FAKERY

Here are some foolproof methods for fossilizing familiar objects, like your dad's slippers. Choose from the following menu of methods, depending on how much time you're prepared to wait:

For quickest results, you could:
- shut them in a deep freeze. This worked well with mammoths in Siberia, which have been deep frozen and perfectly preserved for thousands of years, since

the last Ice Age. Some are so well preserved that one Japanese scientist thinks he can use their frozen cells to recreate baby mammoths. He's busy searching for a suitable mammoth right now.

If you're not in such a hurry, you could:
- hang your dad's slippers under the water that drips from the roof of a limestone cave. The water will be full of dissolved lime, which will soak into the slippers and eventually set like concrete. Come back a few years later and you'll be able to give your dad fossil footwear for his birthday.

For the prettiest results:
- cover them with amber resin, which is formed from the tacky, golden liquid that oozes out of pine trees. When it dries it turns to a transparent yellow stone.

But don't expect rapid results – the amber resin has to fossilize first, and that can take thousands of years. Still, this has worked brilliantly in the past with fossil insects, but you'll need an awful lot of amber to fossilize a pair of slippers.

FOSSILIZED SPIDER IN AMBER, JURASSIC ERA, NEW MEXICO

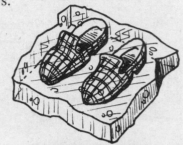

BOB ARKWRIGHT'S SLIPPERS, POST-WAR ERA, GRIMSBY

An even messier method is to:
- dunk the slippers in a pit of thick tar. You can find one of these at Rancho La Brea near Los Angeles in California, where gooey tar bubbles up from below the ground. All sorts of fossil animals have been found perfectly preserved in these pits, even though they fell in thousands of years ago. If it's good enough for sabre-toothed tigers, it's good enough for your dad's slippers.

10,000 YEARS AGO

LAST TUESDAY

But for something really spectacular:

- find an erupting volcano and leave the slippers at the bottom. When Mount Vesuvius in Italy erupted in AD 79 its ash buried the Roman city of Pompeii. Hundreds of people (and slippers) were buried in the ash. It slowly hardened into rock and the bodies (and slippers) rotted away, leaving holes that archaeologists could use like moulds to make plaster casts of the bodies.

SHE'D JUST FETCHED HIS SLIPPERS BEFORE IT ERUPTED

And finally, the method that has worked so well for all sorts of sea creatures:

- chuck the slippers into the sea. When they sink they'll be slowly covered in silt. After a few million years, they should turn to stone – and then some poor palaeontologist in the future will have to spend hours, days, months ... even years, chipping them out again.

HURRY UP – DAD'S FEET ARE COLD

LIVING FOSSILS

Some fossils aren't dead. (You knew that anyway, didn't you? You only need to look at some of your teachers.)

There are plants and animals that are alive today that look exactly like their ancient relatives that were fossilized millions of years ago. Palaeontologists call them "living fossils".

They're brilliant finds because somehow they've survived natural disasters that wiped out most of the creatures and plants that once lived alongside them.

Most fossils only tell us what the tough bits of animals – like shells, bones and teeth – looked like. All the squashy bits, like blood and guts, skin and fur, rot away without becoming fossilized. But living fossils show us what these missing bits looked like, making it easier to imagine what other fossils would be like if you could put the intestines, muscles, brains and other assorted bloody bits back in their original places.

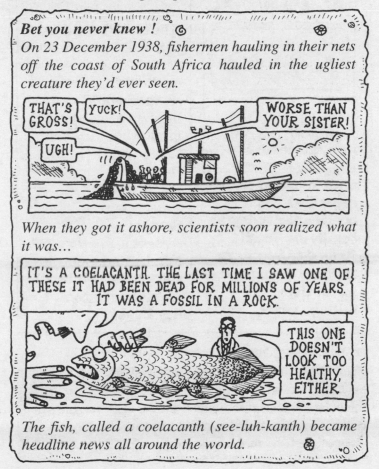

Bet you never knew !
On 23 December 1938, fishermen hauling in their nets off the coast of South Africa hauled in the ugliest creature they'd ever seen.

THAT'S GROSS!

YUCK!

UGH!

WORSE THAN YOUR SISTER!

When they got it ashore, scientists soon realized what it was...

IT'S A COELACANTH. THE LAST TIME I SAW ONE OF THESE IT HAD BEEN DEAD FOR MILLIONS OF YEARS. IT WAS A FOSSIL IN A ROCK.

THIS ONE DOESN'T LOOK TOO HEALTHY, EITHER

The fish, called a coelacanth (see-luh-kanth) became headline news all around the world.

Fintastic FIND!

Fossil

Living specimen

Overjoyed scientists described the coelacanth today as the living fossil find-of-the-century. "It hasn't changed a bit in over 400 million years," said one ecstatic expert, "it's got fantastic fins with bones that support them. About 400 million years ago the fins of fish like this evolved into legs, so they could lumber around on land. "This weird fish is stuck in a time warp. Somehow it's got left behind deep in the ocean, while all its relatives took to dry land."

Dr. C. Lacanth (Fish expert)

FISH FINGERS?

There's a small colony of coelacanths swimming around in the Indian Ocean to this day, but there aren't many left. They might be ugly, but unfortunately they're tasty too. Let's hope coelacanths stay deep down in the ocean, where they belong – out of the fishermen's nets and your fish fingers.

DINOSAUR FARTS: FACTS YOUR TEACHERS ARE TOO EMBARASSED TO TELL YOU

If you think that vegetables in school dinners are hard to digest, spare a thought for vegetarian dinosaurs.

1 They used to eat plants called cycads (sigh-kads), which still survive as living fossils.

2 Cycad leaves are so tough and hard to digest that dinosaurs had to swallow pebbles, to help them grind up the leathery leaves in their gizzards.

SMOOTH PEBBLES

I DON'T KNOW WHAT'S WORSE, EATING THE CYCADS OR THE STONES

3 These gizzard stones, called gastroliths, are often found amongst fossil dinosaur skeletons, in the place where their gizzard was before it rotted away.

4 Some scientists suspect that vegetarian dinosaurs' indigestible diet explains why these animals got to be so big. Their bodies had to contain huge lengths of guts so that the fibrous fronds could slowly go soft inside them.

5 One thing's for sure – the digestion of cycad leaves produced plenty of gas, so dinosaurs would have produced some thunderous farts.

EARTHQUAKE? METEORITE? VOLCANO?

BOOM!

WORSE... DINOSAUR FART!

FANTASTIC FACTS

Living fossils are still being discovered. One of the latest finds is the Wollemi pine, a relative of the monkey puzzle tree. Specimens were first found in a hidden Australian valley in 1994. Some cheeky monkeys have dug some up and pinched a few already. Sadly living fossils, like ordinary fossils, are very popular collector's items.

There are probably loads more living fossils just waiting to be found. Who knows what strange surprises are hidden in dark and dingy corners of the planet?

Species don't last for ever. They all eventually disappear, and are replaced by new ones. You've probably noticed that there are no dinosaurs roaming around in your local nature reserve today. All that's left of them is their fossil bones. So how did they meet their horrible end?

As usual, scientists came up with a whole load of theories, but now they think they know, thanks to a neat piece of detective work.

DINO DOOMSDAY

The disappearance of the dinosaurs is one of evolution's greatest mysteries. Hundreds of species became extinct, all at once. We know this because geologists find their fossils in rocks that were formed up to 65 million years ago, but in later finds, there's not a dinosaur bone to be seen.

While they lived dinosaurs were fantastically successful, and for over 150 million years they dominated almost every habitat. The biggest meat-eating dinosaurs, like *Tyrannosaurus rex*, had no enemies. So why did the fiercest, meanest, most successful animals on Earth suddenly become extinct 65 million years ago?

TEST YOUR TEACHER

Why did the dinosaurs die? Was it because of...

1 Ultra-violent hurricanes (called ultracanes), that whisked dust into the air, blotted out the sun and plunged the planet into a winter that lasted for years, so the dinosaurs died of the cold?

2 Showers of deadly particles called neutrinos (new-tree-nose), released from the explosion of a dying star, called a supernova? The neutrinos caused fatal cancers in the dinosaurs' bodies.

3 A wayward asteroid, cruising through the solar system? The asteroid collided with Earth causing a massive tidal wave, earthquakes and fires that filled the atmosphere with dust and smoke, hiding the sun so that dinosaurs died of cold.

4 Volcanic eruptions in India, that made the atmosphere hellishly hot? The dinosaurs overheated, couldn't lay fertile eggs any more, and died out.

Understanding evolution would be a lot simpler if we could take a trip back in time, so we could witness what went on in the past. So just for a moment, imagine that you and your teacher are time travellers, and that you've been whisked back to that fateful day when the destiny of the dinosaurs was decided...

You're in North America and the land is swarming with dinosaurs. It's the dawn of a summer's morning and you are standing on the edge of a forest of tough cycad plants. It's 65 million BC!

It's been a cold night and most of the dinosaurs are still chilled and sluggish. They yawn, snore and now and then let loose a deafening fart. You're safe for now, as they won't start moving about much until the sun has warmed them up.

Watch where you put your feet, though! There's dinosaur dung all over the place. In 65 million years' time it will have turned into fossilized coprolites, but for now it's squelchy and very, *very* smelly.

This morning, the dinosaurs are unusually restless. There's a distant, pale yellow glow in the eastern sky. In a few minutes the sun will rise, but all eyes that are open are already looking south, towards a brilliant glow in the sky that has been growing brighter every day. It started as a shining speck, months ago, and grew until it looked as large as the moon.

Today it's as bright as the sun that's about to creep over the horizon – and it is rushing towards the Earth like a giant thunderbolt. It's moving towards the Earth's surface at a speed of 9 km (6 miles) per second. It's been wandering through the solar system for millions of years, until at last gravity started to pull it towards our planet.

There is a flash of light hundreds of miles south of where you're standing now. The asteroid has struck at last. All is still and silent as the rising sun begins to strike the leathery hides of the dinosaurs.

At first it seems as though nothing has happened. Then, after several minutes the sound of the distant explosion arrives, as a thunderous, ear-splitting rumble. The dinosaurs struggle to their feet and lumber around in a blind panic. Look out! Dive for cover behind a rock! They'll crush underfoot everything that gets in their way.

The ground trembles and shakes. Earthquakes tear the soil apart, creating yawning chasms big enough to swallow the largest dinosaurs. There are scenes of terrible and total destruction all over Earth. Thousands of square miles of land around the asteroid's crater are lifeless. Great fires sweep across dry grasslands and forests, fanned by howling gales.

At sea, a towering tidal wave over a kilometre high is rolling away from the crater where the asteroid landed. It will engulf islands, washing them clean of life, and then sweep inland over the coasts of continents, drowning anything in its path.

But most frightening of all, a giant mushroom cloud of smoke and dust is already rising into the stratosphere, and spreading. By the middle of the day it will have blotted out the sun, casting the world into a twilight that will last for years. Plants, starved of sunlight, wither and die – very bad news if you're a giant and very hungry plant-eating dinosaur.

You can breathe a sigh of relief now, 'cos you can leap forward in time, back into the twentieth century. Did you remember to remind your teacher to come back with you? I know it's tempting, but...

So **3** – a collision with an asteroid – is the answer that most scientists favour, but how did they work it out? The scientist who came up with the answer was...

Hall of fame: Luis Walter Alvarez (1911–1988)
Nationality: American

Luis Alvarez was a man with a lively mind. He was a physics professor who studied cosmic rays. During the Second World War he invented a kind of radar that let aeroplanes land when the ground was hidden under a blanket of fog. After that he spent his life working out what atoms are made from – and won a Nobel Prize for his discoveries. In his spare time he used X-rays to find out what was inside an Egyptian pyramid, and also found time to figure out what happened to the dinosaurs.

Alvarez and his son, Walter, believed that a giant asteroid collided with Earth 65 million years ago. The awesome asteroid collision sent out a giant tidal wave that swept over islands in the oceans and flooded the edges of the land. It filled the atmosphere with dust and choking gases that spread around the planet, blocking out the sun and plunging Earth into a winter that went on for years.

Several years of continuous winter would have been very bad news for dinosaurs. We mammals generate and store warmth in our bodies from the chemical reactions that break down our food, so our body temperature stays steady even on the coldest days. But dinosaurs were cold-blooded and needed warmth from sunshine to boost their body temperature. They probably spent most of their time lounging around in the sun all day, soaking up the rays.

So once winter set in the cold-blooded dinosaurs started to shiver, and soon died out. The asteroid wiped out three-quarters of all the living things on the planet. The era of the dinosaurs was over. The reign of the warm-blooded mammals, that had survived the catastrophe, was about to begin.

But could it really have happened like this?

FANTASTIC FACTS: CLUES TO A CALAMITOUS COLLISION

- Asteroids collide with planets all the time. The icy centre of a comet that exploded five miles above Tunguska in Siberia in 1908 flattened 1,200 square miles of forest and singed the clothes of people 60 miles away.

*LIVING IN TUNGUSKA IS SO BORING – NOTHING EXCITING EVER HAPPENS

- The solar system is a bit like a 3D snooker table. Sooner or later the smaller lumps of rock that are whizzing around are bound to collide with something big. Our moon is covered with asteroid craters. We can still see them because there's no wind or water up there, to wear them away.
- Geologists have found a monster crater, made by an asteroid about 65 million years ago, in the sea off the Yucatan Peninsula in Mexico. Could this be the big one, that brought doomsday for dinosaurs?

- Any asteroid that made a hole that big would have been 10,000 times more destructive than all the nuclear bombs that have ever been built.
- Asteroids carry a rare element called iridium. There is a layer of dust loaded with iridium covering rocks all over the world that was laid down 65 million years ago. The iridium particles must have settled from the dust cloud after the asteroid struck.

Bet you never knew!
The mass extinction of dinosaurs 65 million years ago is the one that everybody talks about, but it wasn't the only time when life on Earth had nearly been wiped out. About 245 million years ago nearly 96 per cent of all species became extinct. That was doomsday for the trundling trilobites and savage sea scorpions. No one is really sure why that happened. Many scientists believe the planet got hotter, so some of the seas dried up, wiping out animals that lived in shallow water. Also most of the sea creatures that died out had tiny larval stages that began life swimming in the plankton in the surface layers of the sea. So perhaps chemical changes in the sea poisoned them. We'll never know for sure.

Even earlier than this, another mysterious mass extinction wiped out these incredible creatures:

NAME: *Hallucigenia* (Hell-loo-see-gee-knee-ar)

APPEARANCE:
Scientists studying its
fossils have had real
trouble trying to work
out which way up this

animal stood, but now they're pretty sure
that it had seven pairs of legs, a nozzle at one
end and a row of spikes along its back.

DIED OUT: Over 500 million years ago.

NAME: *Opabinia* (O-par-bin-knee-ar)

APPEARANCE: Like a swimming vacuum
cleaner, with five eyes and a nozzle with claws
at one end. Opabinia was a predator that

probably swam along
the sea floor and used
its flexible nozzle to
grab anything that
came too close.

DIED OUT: Over 500 million years ago.

Fortunately, evolution is very good at coming up with
new designs to equip creatures for tough conditions in
a changing world. Some life has always pulled through
after catastrophic mass extinctions. Sometimes it seems
that – if you give it enough time – evolution can invent
just about anything…

FISH WITH FEET

Evolution is very good at inventing new animals without any help from us. Nothing big happens overnight. Each small step can take millions of years. But give it enough time and evolution can come up with some amazing inventions. Take eyes, for example…

It all started with a simple chemical that was sensitive to light.
This was useful because it allowed its owner to tell whether it was:
- out in the open, where it might be eaten by its enemies.
- or under a stone, where it would be safe.

Next, the light detector chemical became concentrated inside a light sensitive patch inside a small pit in the skin, with just a tiny hole letting light in. The result was a kind of camera eye, which could form a picture. It works surprisingly well…

Dare you discover … how to see the world through a pinhole camera?
- Find a tube. Something about 30 cm long and 8 cm wide would be ideal, but the exact size doesn't matter.

- Tape some aluminium foil over one end and prick the tiniest possible hole in the middle with a sharp pin.
- Tape a piece of tracing paper over the other end.
- Then point the pinhole at a bright window or bright light. You'll see an image upside down on the tracing paper. This is how a pinhole camera works. Some snails have got eyes like this.

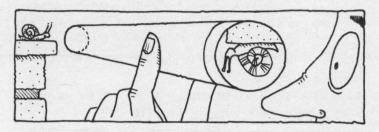

So, now you've seen the world through the eye of a snail. The picture is clear enough to tell you whether that animal lurking outside your home is a friend or an enemy – even if it's upside down.

After that, eyes just got better and better, one step at a time.

- In some animals the pit became filled with jelly that bent the light rays and focused them on to light sensitive cells. So the picture got clearer.

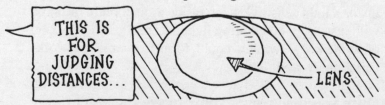

THIS IS FOR JUDGING DISTANCES...

LENS

- Then the jelly hardened into a lens which could be pulled by muscles into different shapes. This focused things that were close up or far away.

- A transparent skin evolved, that covered the delicate eye to protect it.

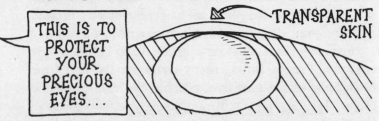

- A pupil evolved inside the eye, to open and close the hole where light entered, so that it worked in bright or dim light.

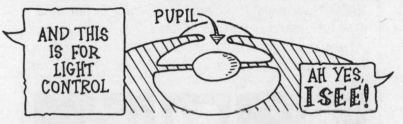

It's taken evolution the best part of 1,000 million years to come up with an eye like ours – but it managed it in the end. And what's even more amazing is that it's done it more than once, in different groups of animals. Squid, which are members of the snail family, have eyes that are almost as good as ours.

CAVE CREATURES

Deep in underground caves there are animals that biologists call troglodytes – species that live in caves all their lives and never come to the surface. Some troglodytes, like the poor old Texas blind salamander, evolved from ancestors that once lived on the surface and had eyes. When they evolved into cave dwellers their eyes gradually disappeared again, because they were useless in total darkness. It's scary living in places like this, and the salamander has to grope its way around, pursuing prey with an extra-sensitive sense of smell.

Imagine what it must have been like to be a biologist exploring one of these creepy caves for the first time. Some blind spiders have evolved a horrible hunting method, feeling for their prey with long dangly legs, before they sink their jaws into its body. You need nerves of steel if you want to explore the eyeless world of the troglodytes.

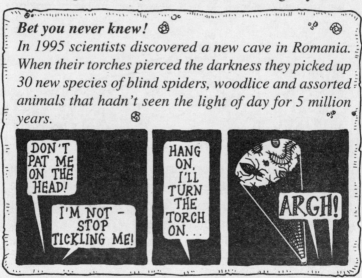

Bet you never knew!
In 1995 scientists discovered a new cave in Romania. When their torches pierced the darkness they picked up 30 new species of blind spiders, woodlice and assorted animals that hadn't seen the light of day for 5 million years.

DON'T PAT ME ON THE HEAD!

I'M NOT – STOP TICKLING ME!

HANG ON, I'LL TURN THE TORCH ON...

ARGH!

TEST YOUR TEACHER
Stygophilic (say sty-go-fill-ik) means:
1 to live in a pig sty.
2 to live in dark caves.
3 a pig that's so fat it can't fit in its sty.

Answer: 2)

102

PTEROSAURS TAKE OFF

Sometimes evolution creates new inventions by taking something that already exists and adapting it so that it can be used for something else.

Back in the Jurassic era, 200 million years ago, it was horribly hot during the day and uncomfortably cool at night. Some small ancestors of pterosaurs found themselves shivering at dawn, after a long cool night, and wilting by lunchtime, when the sun blazed down overhead.

But some of these ancestral pterosaurs evolved a terrific trick for preventing their body temperature from going up and down like a yo-yo. They grew sheets of thin skin full of blood vessels between their limbs and their body, to increase their surface area. This meant they could cool down faster in the day, and spread their wings to catch the first warm rays of the sun at dawn.

On really hot days they might have flapped these sheets of skin to create a cool breeze. And suddenly, they were airborne. Their cooling devices were perfectly pre-adapted to become glider wings.

ONE SMALL STEP FOR FISH...

Remember the coelacanth (see-la-kanth), the living fossil on page 87?

Similar animals crawled out of the sea millions of years ago and evolved into animals that could live in water or on land – they became amphibians, like today's frogs, toads and newts. The coelacanth's bony fins were already well on their way to becoming bony legs.

Of course, climbing out on to land was only half the battle. Fish breathe through gills that are designed to take in oxygen from water, and these aren't much use on land. Clambering out onto dry land would have been a disaster unless they'd already begun to evolve a way of breathing oxygen from air instead of from water. And luckily, they'd done just that.

Today, if you dig down into dried mud in African lake beds in the dry season, you'll find fish. Lung fish. They evolved extra loops in their guts that expanded into lungs, for breathing air. They probably first evolved these extra gut gas-exchangers for living in murky, muddy waters where there wasn't much oxygen. Today they can use them to breathe air when they're buried in a dry lake bed, waiting for the rain to come and fill up their lake again.

So when fish began to scramble out on to land they were already equipped with a primitive kind of lung that allowed them to breath oxygen from air if they gulped it into their gut extensions, which eventually evolved into proper, more efficient lungs.

A WHOLE NEW YOU?

If you look at animals closely enough, you often find that they already have the essential equipment for evolving into something new. Shrink a bit here, stretch a bit there and they can be transformed into something that looks completely different.

These days scientists can transform animals by snipping genes out of one animal and splicing them into another one, to alter the genetic instructions for making its body. It's called genetic engineering.

Who knows, maybe in the future – with a little help from genetic engineers – we'll be able to equip people with some useful new body bits, like…

INFRARED VISION

What's infrared?

Invisible light given out by warm objects.

Who can see it?

Horribly poisonous snakes called pit vipers. They use it to "see" the warm bodies of their prey in total darkness.

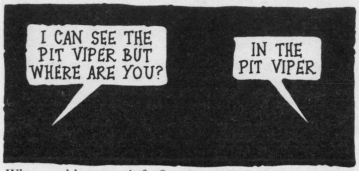

What could we use it for?

You'd never tread on the cat in the dark, for a start. Everyone would emit a warm, rosy glow after dark. And you could go bird-watching at night.

BUILT-IN COMPASSES

What do they do?

They allow some animals to find their way around the world (and get back home again) without using a compass. They're tiny magnetic granules in their brains, that give them a sense of direction.

Who's got them?

Honey-bees and pigeons, for certain, and maybe some other animals too. Pigeons and migrating birds use a built-in compass to find their way home over hundreds of miles of unfamiliar territory.

How would it help us?

You'd never get lost. You'd always know which direction

to walk in, wherever you were, to get home. The bad news would be that you'd never be able to say you got lost when you were late for school.

I THOUGHT YOU SAID YOU HAD THE HOMING INSTINCTS OF A PIGEON, WILKINS

THAT'S WHY I KEEP STAYING AT HOME, SIR

BODY ELECTRICITY

What is it?
Electric charges stored in body muscles.
Who's got it?
Electric eels. They use it to stun their prey.
How would it help us?
You'd never need batteries for your torch again. But you'd need to be very careful when you shook hands.

It's fun trying to imagine how humans could be modified in the future, either by evolution or by genetic engineers, but we're only just beginning to discover what kind of animals we evolved from in the past. Ever since Darwin came up with his theory of evolution, scientists have suspected that monkeys and men share the same ancient ancestors...

NEW KIDS ON THE BLOCK

Today our planet is inhabited by a mixture of old inhabitants and newly evolved arrivals.

Fantastic fact: you can still find bacteria in sulphur springs and around deep-sea volcanoes that are almost identical to fossil bacteria buried in rocks that are three and a half billion years old.

Bet you never knew!

Mosses – those tiny green plants that grow in cracks in pavements and are trodden underfoot without a second thought every day – are incredible survivors. They haven't changed much since they first invaded land, over 500 million years ago. Today's moss species are very similar to the ones that were trodden underfoot by the dinosaurs. They are one of evolution's success stories.

We humans are recent arrivals – the new kids on the block. Will we be as successful and survive as long as sulphur bacteria and mosses? It's too soon to tell. But we can look backwards through the human family photo album and search for clues to one of evolution's most fascinating questions … who were the first humans?

You probably think you've got a pretty good idea what

the first humans looked like, from the pictures that are often drawn in comics. You know the kind of thing...

A SHAMBLING WALK

A FOREHEAD THAT JUTTED OUT OVER THEIR EYES

NO CHIN

LONG ARMS THAT DANGLED SO THAT THEIR KNUCKLES DRAGGED ALONG THE GROUND

Sounds familiar?

That's right. They looked very much like today's PE teachers.

Actually, we can't really be sure what the first humans looked like, because we've only got a few scattered bones to go on. If they were around today the first humans would probably be very upset at being drawn like this in comics (and being compared with PE teachers).

But let's get one thing straight. Whatever you might have heard, humans didn't evolve from chimpanzees, gorillas or PE teachers.

TEST YOUR TEACHER
Pongidae (pon-gid-ee) is:
1 The scientific name for the chimp family.
2 The scientific name for the bacteria in smelly trainers.

3 The breathtaking brand of aftershave used by teachers.

PONGIDAE?   PONGIDAE?   PONGIDAE?

We are very similar to these fine furry apes – and we share most of their genes – but they are not our direct ancestors.

What probably happened was this.

Long ago – maybe as long as four million years – an unknown chimp-like ape lived in Africa. It was probably horribly hairy and probably walked on all four legs.

. . . AND PROBABLY LOOKED LIKE THIS

OOH, OOH AH, AH!

Some of these ancient ancestors evolved into today's chimps. Another branch of the family took off in a different direction, and evolved into hominids – the name the scientists give to the branch of the ape family that humans belong to. Today's chimps will never evolve into humans, however many million years we wait – they're following their own evolutionary path, one that leads away from humans.

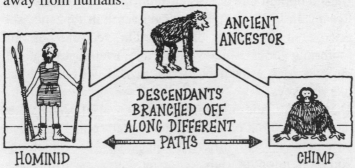

ANCIENT ANCESTOR

DESCENDANTS BRANCHED OFF ALONG DIFFERENT PATHS

HOMINID

CHIMP

For most of this century scientists have been trying to find remains of our mysterious, extinct hominid ancestors – the missing links in the evolutionary story – who left the trees and walked upright across the African Plains.

This, for example is Australopithecus (Os-tral-o-pith-e-cus), whose name means "southern ape". He lived about four million years ago.

AUSTRALOPITHECUS

NOT TO BE CONFUSED WITH MR BROWN SCIENCE TEACHER

WALK TALL

The first person to prove that our ancient ancestors walked upright like us was an anthropologist called Mary Leakey. In 1976, at a place called Laetoli in Tanzania, she discovered three trails of 3.6-million-year-old hominid footprints – rock-solid evidence that, even that long ago, our ancestors walked on two legs, and not on all fours like monkeys.

So what made humans decide to walk upright, after they'd started out padding around on all fours? Scientists have come up with different suggestions. See which one you think might be right.

1 Walking on two legs helped humans to lose heat in hot climates. Standing up straight meant they exposed less of their body to the scorching African sun and might have helped keep their heads and brains cool.

2 Or it might have been for protection. If they stood up straight, maybe they could see predators coming more easily? Life for early hominids could be horribly hazardous.

3 Frees the hands for making and using tools.

In 1924 a group of palaeontologists working in Taung, South Africa unearthed a pile of bones. They were able to work out that the bones were about 3 million years old and belonged to several small animals. Most of the bones came from rat-like creatures, but some bones looked strangely familiar. When they looked more closely, they discovered that these bones belonged to a child. But this child wouldn't have looked anything like you do. This child belonged to an early species of hominid, called *Australopithecus africanus*. He seems to have come to a horrible end. But how did it happen?

a) Was he pounced on by a pack of rats and did he die fighting them off, killing several in the struggle?

b) Was he buried alongside the family pets, after he died of natural causes?

c) Or was he killed by an eagle, that cut him up into pieces with its fearsome beak and carried him back in bite-sized chunks to its nest, to feed its chicks.

LUCY OR LUCIAN?

Scientists tend to get very wrapped up in their work. When they find a particularly interesting specimen, they can really get quite attached to it. Sometimes they might even give it a name.

This happened when a well-preserved specimen was found, piece by piece, in the 1970s in Ethiopia. It was a female member of a hominid called *Australopithecus afarensis* (which means "southern ape from the Afar region of Ethiopia"). Like us, she walked upright but when she was fully grown she was no bigger than an average 12-year-old child today – about 1.3 metres tall.

She was such a fantastic specimen that she got herself a name: Lucy, after the Beatles song, "Lucy in the Sky with Diamonds".

More recently a question has arisen about Lucy. She might not be a girl after all. After 3 million years it's

114

hard to tell. So will Lucy have to be renamed Lucian?
Scientists are still arguing about that one.

LUVERLY LATIN

I bet you're wondering where all these strange, tongue-twisting scientific names come from.

Scientists give all living things a name written in Latin, the language of the ancient Romans. This is because Latin names are understood by all scientists, everywhere. If the names were written in English or Chinese or Spanish, they wouldn't mean much to people who didn't speak those languages.

Latin names come in two parts. The first part is called the genus and the second part is the species. There are often dozens of different species in a genus. For example, there are several different kinds of   They're all in the genus *Panthera*, but each one   species name, so…

- *Panthera tigris* is the tige
- *Panthera leo* is the lion
- *Panthera pardus* is th African leo
- *Panthera onca* is th

If the Pink Panth
Panthera rosea.

Latin names usually tell you something about their owners. So…

Once human evolution got into its stride, a whole series of hopeful hominids appeared on the scene. It's time to meet a few relatives you didn't know you had:

HANDYMAN

NAME: *Homo habilis* (which means "tool-making man").

AGE: Lived between one and a half and two million years ago.

LAST KNOWN ADDRESS: First found by Mary Leakey in Africa, alongside the bones of lots of our other relatives.

APPEARANCE: Hard to say, because scientists have only found a few bones. But probably very hairy, and walked upright.

BEST KNOWN FOR: Inventing stone tools. Humans were starting to get clever.

FIRE MAN

NAME: Could be another member of the species *Homo erectus* (the species lasted a long time), although some scientists have given him the more impressive name of *Homo heidelburgensis*, because suspiciously similar bones have been dug up around Heidelburg in Germany.

AGE: First appeared about one and a half million years ago.

LAST KNOWN ADDRESS: Africa, Asia and Europe.

APPEARANCE: Taller, and larger brain than *Homo habilis*.

BEST KNOWN FOR: Setting fire to things. The first hominid to use fire.

BOXGROVE MAN

NAME: *Homo heidelbergensis*. Seen by some scientists as another kind of *Homo erectus*.

AGE: Oldest known Englishman – is 450,000 years old. May have still been around 30,000 years ago in some parts of the world.

LAST KNOWN ADDRESS: Boxgrove in Sussex, England.

APPEARANCE: Hard to tell. A jaw bone was found near Heidelburg. Then archaeologists found a few teeth and a leg bone in 1995. That's not a lot to go on.

BEST KNOWN FOR: Butchery. His remains were found amongst rhinoceros bones that probably belonged to one that he skinned and ate (rhinoceros lived in Britain before Ice Ages drove them further south).

NEANDERTHAL MAN

NAME: *Homo neandertalensis* (which means "wise man, from the Neander valley in Germany").

AGE: Was still around in Europe until about 30,000 years ago.

LAST KNOWN ADDRESS: Lived in several places in Western Europe.

BEST KNOWN FOR: Living in caves. Probably far more intelligent than we gave them credit for. They had bigger brains than us, for a start.

WISE MAN

NAME: *Homo sapiens* (which means "wise man"). And that means you. You are a member of this species.

AGE: About 250,000 years.

ADDRESS: Everywhere.

BEST KNOWN FOR: Outrageous behaviour.

Until the 1950s, scientists believed there was another type of hominid roaming around on Earth about 200,000 years ago. His name was Piltdown Man, because his skull was found in Piltdown, Sussex in England. He was discovered in 1908.

Chemical tests finally proved that Piltdown Man was a complete hoax! His skull was made by glueing together broken pieces of skulls from a variety of skeletons. No one is absolutely certain to this day who made a monkey out of so many scientists, but there have been all sorts of theories.

*Some say the forger was Charles Dawson, the amateur geologist who first unearthed the skull. Others point the finger at Sir Arthur Conan Doyle, the author and creator of Sherlock Holmes. Conan Doyle was a keen amateur bone hunter who lived just next door to the quarry where the skull was found, **and** he once wrote a book called* The Lost World *where forged fossils play a part in the plot.*

ABOMINABLE BUT TRUE?

In the last century Chinese scientists made a remarkable discovery. They found strange items on sale in Chinese markets, labelled "dragon's teeth". The scientists soon proved that these teeth were actually fossilized teeth of a giant, gorilla-like animal. More teeth were discovered in caves, alongside some outsized skeletons.

The scientists were able to prove that, once upon a time, something like a million years ago, there lived a monster ape, who was almost twice as big as today's humans. Scientists called the creature *Gigantopithecus* (Jy-gan-toe-pith-ikus) – which means giant ape. Could that be how myths about giants have come about? Was the American Bigfoot, or the Abominable Snowman of the Himalayas really *Gigantopithecus*? And does it still exist?

We may never find an Abominable Snowman, but finding all the other species that exist today is a high priority for scientists. And that's turning out to be a major problem, because if you don't know a species exists, how do you know what to look for...?

WHAT ELSE IS OUT THERE?

It's surprising how easily scientists can overlook large animals. You might think that they would have found all the most spectacular creatures long ago, but new ones keep turning up.

So how on earth did scientists manage to miss…

MEGAMOUTH SHARKS

(*Megachasma pelagios* – which means "great yawning mouth of the open sea")

FIRST FOUND: Caught accidentally by a research ship off Hawaii in 1976. No more seen until another one turned up off the Californian coast in 1983. Since then a few more have been seen around Australia and Japan.

QUICK! IN HERE!

FINEST FEATURES: The sixth largest shark in the world, five metres long, with a massive mouth. Seems surprisingly friendly, even though it has 400 teeth arranged in 236 rows. Luckily, they're all very small. The inside of its mouth glows in the dark and biologists believe that it cruises around in the deep ocean with its mouth open, looking like a predatory torch and inviting minute marine life to swim towards the glow.

As an added treat, scientists have also discovered a new kind of parasitic worm that lives in megamouth's guts.

FUTURE PROSPECTS: Not too bad. They're shy – always a good policy when humans are around. Mention the word "shark" and most people reach for a harpoon.

And who'd have thought that we could overlook something as large as…

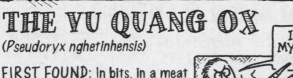

THE VU QUANG OX

(Pseudoryx nghetinhensis)

FIRST FOUND: In bits, in a meat market in Vietnam, in 1992. Local people already knew what it looked like (and how to cook it). Living specimens not seen by Western scientists until 1994.

FINEST FEATURES: About as big as a goat, with extremely handsome horns.

FUTURE PROSPECTS: Succulent meat, so the Vu Quang's future might not be too bright. And those horns would make a tempting hunter's trophy . . .

And why did it take so long to find…

ASTBESTOPLUMA SPONGE

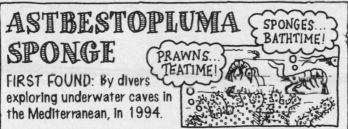

FIRST FOUND: By divers exploring underwater caves in the Mediterranean, in 1994.

FINEST FEATURES: The world's only meat-eating sponge. Seems to like eating small prawns. It catches them with hooks on tiny tentacles all over its surface – they work like Velcro, snaring anything that blunders into them.

FUTURE PROSPECTS: Murky. The Mediterranean is horribly polluted, so it may not survive.

And, although we've probably been eating them for years, scientists failed to spot the tiny…

SYMBION PANDORA

> I'M QUITE ATTACHED TO THEM, REALLY!

FIRST FOUND: Attached to the mouths of Norwegian lobsters in 1995.

FINEST FEATURES: A small animal, only one millimetre long, but a mega discovery. *Symbion* is a Cyclophoran (Sy-klee-off-or-ran) – a completely new, major group of animals that are unlike anything else on Earth. Males spend their whole lives perched on females. Both can rebuild parts of their bodies if they get damaged.

FUTURE PROSPECTS: Depends on how well Norwegian lobsters do, really, because *Symbion* is permanently attached to their mouths. People eat Norwegian lobsters, so they've been eating *Symbion* for years, without realizing it.

Look closely, and who knows what weird and wonderful creatures might be lurking in unexplored parts of the world? Although scientists have been exploring the Earth for centuries in their search for new species, they've still only found a tiny fraction of the total number that live on the planet.

COUNTING SPECIES
We share our planet with vast numbers of other kinds of plants and animals. Have you any idea how many species exist?

Try asking your teacher first. Are there:
a) 1 million?
b) 10 million?

c) 30 million?
d) 100 million?

Answer: No one really knows. So far biologists have found and described about one and a half million, but they all agree (for once!) that there must be many more. One of the scientists who's tried harder than most to search out new species is an American beetle expert, called Terry Erwin.

Erwin carried out a devastatingly simple experiment. He covered a tree called *Luehia seemannii* in the Panamanian rain forest with smoke and collected all the dazed beetles that fell out of its branches.

He found over 160 undiscovered beetle species amongst the pile of beetles that collected around his feet. He knew that there are about 50,000 different species of tropical rain forest tree, so Terry did a few simple sums to work out how many more undiscovered beetles might be hiding in rain forests.

Terry Erwin was only looking at beetles. If there are 8 million of them, how many other insects might there be?

How many worms, snails and other creepy-crawlies, not to mention fungi, plants and bacteria, are there? Not long ago, researchers in Norway dug up 4,000 new species of bacteria in a single teaspoonful of soil.

So if your teacher guessed that 100 million species was the answer, they might be right. (Don't tell them, though. Teachers can get cocky if they think they're right all the time.)

Today, sadly, extinctions are happening faster and faster, and man is mostly to blame. Many of the best habitats are being destroyed by man through pollution or to make way for new homes, industries and farmlands. So far we humans haven't been too clever when it comes to conserving biodiversity. One way or another, we are wiping out thousands of species. So spare a thought for:

- The dodo. Once lived on the tiny island of Mauritius in the Indian Ocean. It was especially happy because it had no enemies on the island. Until, of course, man arrived and brought rats, cats and dogs. The poor old dodo had no wings, so it couldn't fly off. The last dodo was so slow, it bit the dust as long ago as 1680.
- Steller's sea cow. A tame and gentle creature. Named after George Steller, a German naturalist who discovered the sea cow when he was shipwrecked in 1742. The last sea cow was spotted in 1769, and it followed the fate of the rest of its family ... to be eaten by sailors.
- The passenger pigeon. In the early 1800s the skies above the American forests were filled with passenger pigeons, as they flew in flocks up to 300 million strong.

Incredibly, by 1914 there was only one passenger pigeon left. Passenger pigeons had been hunted down for food and the forests where they nested were destroyed. Each pair of birds only laid a single egg each year, so farmers simply killed them faster than they could breed. When the last passenger pigeon popped off its perch in Cincinnati Zoo the species was finally finished.

- The Tasmanian wolf looked like a smaller, slimmer version of the European wolf, but was striped and used to carry its babies in a pouch, like a kangaroo. Sheep farmers on the island of Tasmania were furious when it took a fancy to their flocks, so they wiped it out. The last survivor died in Hobart Zoo in 1936.
- The dusky seaside sparrow. Once upon a time, the Cape Kennedy space centre was just a vast stretch of marshland. It was a sparrow's paradise. But then the rockets went up, and the bird's came down as the development of the site wiped out their food supply. Scientists couldn't save them, and this sparrow made its final flight in 1984.

Tasmanian wolf
R.I.P. 1936
WIPED OUT FOR WOLFING SHEEP

Dusky Seaside Sparrow
R.I.P. 1984
ROCKETS TOOK THEIR SPACE

EPILOGUE

Nothing can bring back extinct species, but there's still time to save tigers, Spix's macaw, the Californian condor, the Madagascan serpent eagle, the ivory-billed woodpecker, the hawksbill turtle and the giant panda, which are all sliding towards extinction...

One thing is certain. It's taken a horribly long time for them to evolve, so scientists aren't going to let them disappear without a fight.

EVOLVE OR DIE

QUIZ

**Now find out if you're an
Evolve or Die expert!**

Prove it!

So, do you think you've got the gist of genes and understood evolution? Take these quick quizzes and find out if you are a true Homo sapiens ("wise man") or nothing more than a moronic monkey.

GRIPPING GENES

The discovery of genes opened up a whole new world of understanding the human body. It was as though strange scientists had suddenly mastered the meaning of life. But what are these peculiar particles, and just why are they so important? Take this quick quiz and find out.

1 What role do genes play in the human body?
a) They create blood cells.
b) They control inherited characteristics.
c) No one knows…

2 What happens when a dominant gene and a recessive gene combine in offspring?

a) The characteristics of both genes combine to make a hybrid.

b) The characteristic of the recessive gene show.

c) The characteristics of the dominant gene show.

3 What is the name of the body bit that carries your genes?

a) Chromosome

b) Metronome

c) Garden gnome

4 What is the name given to the process by which genes change naturally?

a) Genetics

b) Mutation

c) Alteration

5 How long does it take for one human cell to completely copy its DNA?

a) Eight hours

b) One year

c) Your whole lifetime

6 How many pairs of chromosomes are found in each cell of the human body?

a) 23

b) 46

c) 2

7 What human cells don't have this number of chromosomes?
a) Egg and sperm cells
b) Hair cells
c) Skin cells

8 Which of the following statements is true?
a) Goldfish have the same number of chromosomes as humans.
b) Goldfish have more chromosomes than humans.
c) Goldfish have few chromosomes than humans.

Answers:
1b; 2c; 3a; 4b; 5a; 6a; 7a (Egg and sperm cells have 23 chromosomes each – not 23 pairs); **8b**

DOTTY DARWIN

Old Charles Darwin turned beliefs about the origin of living things upside down with his theory of evolution. Can you tell which of the following statements about the nutty naturalist are true and which are false?

1 Darwin originally studied medicine but dropped out to study theology (religion) instead.
2 Crazy Charles married his niece, Emma Wedgewood.
3 On the journey back from the Galapagos Islands, Darwin and others on board the Beagle ate all the giant tortoises they had collected as a tasty meal.
4 Other than tempting tortoises, Darwin was actually a very fussy eater.
5 Darwin suffered badly from seasickness throughout the whole five-year voyage of the Beagle.
6 Darwin tried to create flying tortoises by breeding them with birds.
7 When his book On the Origin of Species was published, Darwin thought that the 1,250 copies of the original print run was way too many.
8 Darwin took 20 years to publish his book.

Answers:
1 True. As it turned out, he didn't like theology much either (even though his dad hoped he'd become a clergyman).
2 False. Emma was actually his first cousin.
3 True. Having tucked into the tortoises, greedy Darwin was left with only their shells to study.
4 False. Even as a student Darwin had a passion for the unusual, and presided over "The Glutton Club", which met every week to eat "strange flesh" (like hawks and owls).
5 True. Charles chucked up A LOT.
6 False. Although legend has it he once tried to create flying monkeys by breeding them with vultures!

7 True. He was horribly wrong about that though – every copy of the book sold on the first day!
8 True. He knew that religious people would be mighty mad at his suggestions so he kept mum.

UNDERSTANDING EVOLUTION

It took strange scientists hundreds of years to understand evolution, so journey through this potted history of dramatic discovery and see how much you've grasped.

1 What do geologists study? (Clue: The answer will rock your world.)
2 What do scientists use to study the evolution of prehistoric plants and animals? (Clue: It remains to be seen.)
3 What event is believed to have killed the dinosaurs 65 million years ago? (Clue: It had a big impact.)
4 Which group of animals does the term Homo sapiens cover? (Clue: They're very wise animals.)
5 What are the names of the chromosomes in reproductive cells that that control the sex of offspring? (Clue: Not quite Z.)
6 What happens to the chromosomes inside a cell when the cell splits? (Clue: Divide and conquer.)

7 What did Watson and Crick discover in 1953?
(Clue: Do Not Answer?)

Answers:
1 Rocks (including things like fossils).
2 Fossils – the remains of ancient plants and animals.
3 An asteroid hitting the Earth.
4 Humans.
5 X and Y chromosomes. Boys have an X and a Y chromosome; girls have a pair of X chromosomes.
6 The chromosomes also divide so each new cell still has a full set of instructions.
7 The structure of DNA.

EVOLUTION INSIDE OUT

So, have you worked out evolution from the inside out? Put these beastly body bits in order of size with the smallest first, like a set of Russian dolls...

a) DNA
b) Cells
c) Chemical bases
d) Body
e) Genes
g) Chromosomes
f) Nucleus

Answers:
1 c) Chemical bases, which make up…
2 e) Genes, which are units of…
3 a) DNA, which makes up…
4 g) Chromosomes, which can be found in the…
5 f) Nucleus, which is the middle of…
6 b) Cells, which form the…
7 d) Body

GREGOR MENDEL AND HIS GIANT GENE DISCOVERY

Mad monk Mendel was the man who discovered genes (although he didn't call them that). His careful experiments started a new science called genetics – all by messing about with some plants in the monastery garden! See if you can figure out his explanation to his abbot by filling in the missing words.

Dear Abbot,

I am writing to tell you of a most interesting discovery I made while playing with my 1_____ plants. There I was, admiring all the different 2_____, when I started wondering what determined such 3 _____. I began to experiment by carefully 4_____ different types of plants to see what happened. I found that each characteristic is passed on by a tiny 5_____. And these always come in 6 _____. Some are 7_____, which means that their characteristics will always show in the offspring. Others are 8_____, which means that their characteristics can be hidden by a dominant one. I'm sure you'll agree that for a gardener I make a pretty good scientist, and for years to come people will remember how I founded a new branch of science... Do I deserve a promotion?

Yours sincerely,
Brother Mendel

a) cross-pollinating
b) Colours
c) Dominant
d) Pea
e) Particle
f) Pairs
g) Characteristics
h) Recessive

Answers:
1d; 2b; 3g; 4a; 5e; 6f; 7c; 8h

HORRIBLE INDEX

141

HORRIBLE SCIENCE
NASTY NATURE

I LOVE FAST FOOD!

NICK ARNOLD *illustrated by* TONY DE SAULLES

ISBN 978 0439 94451 9

HORRIBLE SCIENCE
DISGUSTING DIGESTION

IT TAKES GUTS!

NICK ARNOLD *illustrated by* TONY DE SAULLES

ISBN 978 0439 94445 8

HORRIBLE SCIENCE
UGLY BUGS

NOT A PRETTY SIGHT!

NICK ARNOLD *illustrated by* TONY DE SAULLES

ISBN 978 0439 94452 6